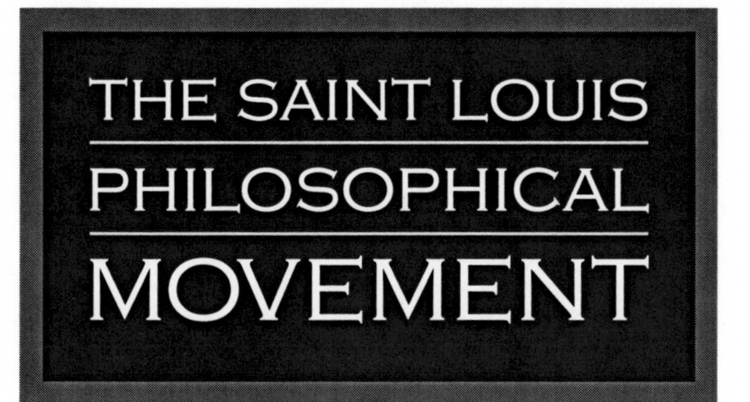

Edited by Britt-Marie Schiller

Cover photographs courtesy Missouri History Museum

Webster University Press
470 East Lockwood Avenue
St. Louis, MO 63119-3194

Library of Congress Control Number: on file

ISBN: 978-0-9821615-1-7

Cover images: Henry Brokmeyer (at left) and William Torrey Harris (at right) are courtesy the Missouri History Museum.

Printed in the United States of America
9 10 11 12 13 5 4 3 2 1

Contents

Foreword

David Carl Wilson, Dean, College of Arts and Sciences, Webster University

Soon after moving from Los Angeles to St. Louis's Webster University as a dean and philosopher in 2002, I was browsing through the philosophy section of Powell's bookstore on the south side of Chicago. Well above my reach I saw three red leather-bound volumes titled *The St. Louis Hegelians*. I perched myself high on a ladder and browsed through the volumes in fascination. St. Louis did not immediately come to mind when thinking about important philosophical movements. Certainly Athens, New England, Vienna, Frankfurt—the list could go on at great length. But St. Louis?

Yet, a century and a half ago, one of the most intense, lively, and unusual philosophical movements in history took root in St. Louis. Perhaps somewhat lacking in modesty, the leaders referred to themselves as "The St. Louis Movement in Philosophy, Literature, and Education." It was a time when the city's leadership comprised four significant threads: transplanted New Englanders, German immigrants, northerly drifting Southerners, and French descendants of the city's founders. This movement blended two of these threads. The New Englanders were represented by the sophisticated William Torrey Harris, and the Germans were represented by the incomparable Henry Conrad Brokmeyer.

They met at a downtown St. Louis lecture in 1858 and discovered their shared interests in German philosophy, New England Transcendentalism, education, and social change. They set up the Kant Club, ostensibly a discussion group but, at the same time, so committed to social engagement that the club played a role in an early Union victory at Camp Jackson. The Kant Club eventually evolved into the St. Louis Philosophical Society, which launched the first English-language philosophical journal in the world, the *Journal of Speculative Philosophy.* Alas, as one writer puts it, "By 1890, however, the St. Louis Movement was as dated as St. Louis's pretensions to future greatness, and the philosophers retained only a unique ability to annoy the young."[1]

Although these philosophers did not generate novel philosophical ideas that changed the course of philosophy, their journal did play a critical role in disseminating groundbreaking ideas by publishing the early works of James, Peirce, and Dewey. And they continue to be of interest owing to their role in the development of American philosophy and their role in the history of the St. Louis region.

But, most important, Harris, Brokmeyer, and other members of the St. Louis Movement are worthy of our close attention because of their commitment to the notion that philosophy must be brought to bear upon life and upon society. Their commitment to education made a direct contribution to the beginnings and growth of the American kindergarten movement. They are credited with contributing to the pioneering commitment of Joseph Pulitzer—a leading St. Louisan of the time—to the importance of investigative journalism. They are credited with contributing to Missouri's critical antislavery and pro-Union stance during the war. They were no less abstract and intellectual than the most bookish of technical philosophers, but they insisted that thought be married to action. Edification, they believed, must be the outcome of philosophy. In this way, they are models to us all.

Sitting atop that ladder, the date 1858 seemed promising. I determined to go back to St. Louis and propose to my colleagues in Webster's philosophy department that we host a celebration of the sesquicentennial of the beginning of the St. Louis Philosophical Movement. Professor Don Morse organized an outstanding conference in 2008, held only a block away from the downtown St. Louis location of Harris and Brokmeyer's initial meeting. This volume, ably edited by Professor Britt-Marie Schiller, grew out of that conference.

As for those three red volumes from Powell's bookstore, they are now among the holdings of Webster University's Emerson Library—immediately beside a copy of the volume you are about to have the great pleasure of reading.

Notes

1. Max Putzel, *The Man in the Mirror* (Columbia: University of Missouri Press, 1998), p. 56.

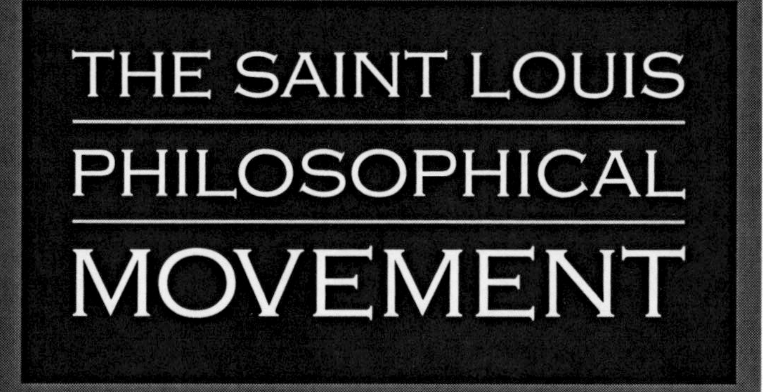
THE SAINT LOUIS
PHILOSOPHICAL
MOVEMENT

Introduction

Britt-Marie Schiller, Webster University

In April 2008, the Philosophy Department at Webster University organized a conference to commemorate the sesquicentennial of the meeting of Henry C. Brokmeyer and William T. Harris at the St. Louis Mercantile Library. After the initial meeting in 1858, these two men embarked on a project that was to shape the St. Louis Philosophical Movement, a systematic study of German idealism, and in particular an interpretation of Hegel's work. While Brokmeyer served as a colonel in the Union Army, during the Civil War Harris kept the small group of Hegel enthusiasts together in St. Louis. Denton J. Snider, a graduate of Oberlin College who had come to St. Louis in 1865 to teach at the Christian Brothers College, joined the group. He became the self-appointed historian of the St. Louis Movement. These three were to form the inner circle of the St. Louis Hegelians. The St. Louis Philosophical Society was formally founded in 1866 and its journal, the *Journal of Speculative Philosophy (JSP)*, the first truly philosophical journal in the United States, was published in 1867. While Brokmeyer spent the rest of his life translating Hegel's *Wissenschaft der Logik*, Harris and Snider were, as the papers in this volume show and attest to, the intellectual forces behind the St. Louis Movement. Taken together they draw a multifaceted, layered portrait of the development of a distinctive American philosophy, pragmatism, and its lasting impact on American culture, intellectual thought, and social institutions.

James A. Good's paper, "The St. Louis Hegelians and the Lost *Bildung* Tradition in American Philosophy," focuses on *Bildung,* the conception of philosophy espoused by the founders of the *JSP*. The St. Louis Philosophical Movement conceptualized philosophy as a fundamentally practical activity, an edifying philosophy, based on Hegel's philosophy of education. The ideal of *Bildung* was to become a self-directed and self-formed person, a person of cultivation and taste. But it went beyond the individual and was used in efforts to reform and promote a progressive society. An example of such a use of philosophy (to solve practical social problems) is the organization of the first kindergarten program in 1873 by Susan Blow and William Harris. Harris subsequently served as superintendent of the St. Louis public schools for twelve years, 1868–80, and as the first United States commissioner of education in 1889. The kindergarten movement grew under Blow's leadership and led to the formation of the New York Kindergarten Association. The *JSP* was an important tool in the effort to reform society and culture. It sought to promote an American type of speculative philosophy, a philosophy that goes beyond epistemology in favor of *Bildung*, edifying and practical philosophy.

In his paper, "St. Louis Hegelians and New England Pragmatists," Douglas Anderson shows the impact of the St. Louis Movement on American pragmatist philosophy, specifically its relation to William James and Charles Sanders Peirce. Both published in the *JSP*, as did John Dewey; hence all three corresponded with William Harris, the editor. Harris's response to Peirce's essay "Nominalism vs. Realism" acted as a catalyst to Peirce's examination of the nature of reality. Anderson argues that, while Peirce's idealism has an important kinship with the views of the St. Louis Movement, his resistance to Hegel's and Harris's reduction of the concrete, the brute element of the universe, to an unchangeable essence residing in the "Forms of Eternity" led him, as a pragmatic idealist, to work on a synthesis of idealism and common sense and to maintain a dialectical tension between speculation and common sense.

The influence of the St. Louis Movement on James was more indirect. Thomas Davidson and George Holmes Howison, who spent time with the St. Louis Hegelians, were both good friends of James. Howison, who developed the philosophy program at University of California–Berkeley, critiqued James's views as too closely allied with features of idealism and revealed to him a way of synthesizing pragmatism and idealism. Davidson was an independent, renegade scholar who believed that universities imprisoned, rather than helped develop, one's thoughts. He, as the St. Louis Hegelians, sought to relate philosophy to culture, and Davidson influenced James in many conversations to ally himself more with working-class people. Davidson and James were committed both to individualism and to pluralism, and both championed the individual will in the transformation of self and culture.

Anderson shows the importance of idealism in pragmatic thought, in particular that pragmatism did not appear out of nowhere. The St. Louis Movement left a permanent trace in American pragmatism.

Jerome P. Schiller shows how strong the strain of idealism was in American pragmatism. In focusing on the metaphysical aspect of Hegelian idealism in the St. Louis Movement in his essay, "William T. Harris on 'The Speculative,'" he offers a close textual analysis of Harris's notion of the concept. He draws on Harris's articles in the *JSP*, the first of which is called "The Speculative," in order to determine just what Harris meant by the Speculative. Harris characterized the world as comprised of three levels of consciousness—the sensory, the imaginative, and the rational—to which correspond the fragmented world of sense, the unified world of science, and the realm of self-determination, respectively. The multiple relations between these are captured in logico-grammatical terms, like mediation, comprehension, and the universal. Ultimately the speculative standpoint was for Harris a self-determination issuing from a self-relation that is conscious of the principles of the speculative system, in addition to being able to evolve such a system, i.e., the highest realm of consciousness.

Another side of William T. Harris emerges in the portrait drawn by Dorothy Rogers in her paper, "Mentor as Blessing/Curse: Marietta Kies and the Problem of Derivative Identity." Harris was an egalitarian who provided opportunities for intellectual women to flourish, among them Susan Blow and Anna Brackett, a feminist and the first woman in the country to head a secondary school. Marietta Kies was one of his students at the Concord Summer School of Philosophy and Literature in Massachusetts. She became the seventh American woman to earn a Ph.D. in philosophy and one of three women to teach philosophy at a co-educational college or university (Butler College in Indianapolis) before 1900.

Kies published *An Introduction to the Study of Philosophy* in 1889, a presentation of Harris's work that won acclaim for its systematic and clear nature. Anticipating feminist care ethics by almost one hundred years, Kies developed a theory of altruism in the 1890s. She argued that, in a truly rational state, justice and grace must complement each other in all realms of human activity. In spite of the originality of her theory of altruism, it was considered derivative of Harris's work, which Rogers attributes to the blessing and the curse of a woman's being the disciple of a prominent man in her field.

The last paper in this collection shows how the St. Louis Hegelians used Hegel's historical dialectic to explain what they saw as a crucial flaw in the American character, intellectual immaturity and unreflective custom. In "Absolute Speculation: The St. Louis Hegelians and the Question of American National Identity," Matt Erlin argues that the appeal of the Hegelian dialectic to the St. Louis Hegelians was that its framework could be used to recontextualize the crisis in American institutions following the Civil War as a step toward the actualization of the country's historical mission. Denton Snider recast Hegel's history of civilization as the history of the American republic, in terms of the achievement of a self-conscious awareness of freedom as the essence of humanity. The disintegration of social institutions was seen as a result of the conflict between individual consciousness and national authority, manifest in the contradictions of slavery. Snider used Hegel's conceptual framework to reconcile his belief in an American mission with the degeneration of political culture in the aftermath of the Civil War.

Viewing the American intellectual deficiency also in comparison to the European intellectual tradition, Snider recognized the shortcoming, but used Hegel's framework to assert America's superiority over Europe in its realization of a constitutional confederacy. The United States then could appear as both more and less advanced than Europe in its realization of an ideal of which its citizenry was still unaware.

Harris entertained a concern similar to Snider's in characterizing the country's moral collapse and the role of education to resolve it. While Snider's focus was institutional, Harris framed his concern in terms of race. He argued that the United States developed according to the principles of an Anglo-Saxon race that lacked a propensity for deep thought. Its strength lay in the establishment of practical institutions, though without the mastery of systematic thought. This aspect was characteristic, however, of German science, which Snider saw as necessary to the development of culture in the United States. Both Harris and Snider, then, used Hegel's framework to rationalize America's moral decline and its lack of a theoretical culture as a temporary phase in the development of the nation.

Erlin concludes that Harris's and Snider's projects, seen from the perspective of the idea of self-consciousness and American intellectual inferiority, must be viewed as a conscious strategy of nation building designed to overcome the latter. The context of a dialectic allowed them to recognize the intellectual immaturity without admitting any permanent inferiority in the American national character.

While the presence of German idealism is strong, the lasting impact of a conception of philosophy as a practical and edifying enterprise emerges clearly in these essays, and in the St. Louis Philosophical Movement's originating contribution to American pragmatist philosophy.

The St. Louis Hegelians and the Lost *Bildung* Tradition in American Philosophy

*James A. Good, Lone Star College—North Harris, Houston**

In 1910, Morris Raphael Cohen, distinguished American philosopher at New York City College, divided the history of modern American philosophy into three periods. According to Cohen's scheme, the three periods corresponded to three philosophical journals, the *Journal of Speculative Philosophy*, established in St. Louis in 1867; the *Philosophical Review*, established at Cornell University in 1892; and the *Journal of Philosophy, Psychology, and Scientific Methods*, founded at Columbia University in 1904. Cohen labeled these three periods of modern American philosophy "the theologic, the metaphysical, and the scientific." Though I question the adequacy of Cohen's labels for these periods, he was certainly correct that American philosophy had become increasingly secular. But Cohen suggested a better way to understand the first period when he noted that, unlike the latter two journals, the *JSP* was founded not by university professors, but by "practical men who believed they had found [a] superior point of view, fruitful insight into the fields of religion, art, history, education, and even practical politics."[1]

It has not been easy for scholars to accurately characterize the *JSP*, nor have scholars adequately understood the thought of the St. Louis Hegelians who founded and operated it until its demise in 1893. This misunderstanding is due to the fact that the St. Louis Hegelians held

* "The St. Louis Hegelians and the Lost Bildung Tradition in American Philosophy" by James A. Good. First published The Journal of Speculative Philosophy (1867-93). 22 volumes. Bristol, U.K.: Thoemmes Press, 2002. Reprinted by permission.

a conception of philosophy that is largely lost today. For the St. Louis Hegelians, philosophy not only addressed the problems of philosophers; it gave meaning to the lives of individuals and unity to society.

Cohen actually provides us with an important example that will clarify this conception of philosophy. In 1899 he encountered Thomas Davidson, a prominent St. Louis Hegelian, and his life was quite literally transformed, and perhaps even saved.[2] Just seven years before, Cohen's family had fled poverty and anti-Semitism in the ghetto of Minsk, Russia, for the impoverished Lower East Side of New York City. Though he considered America a "blessed land of opportunity," as a child in Minsk he had contemplated suicide. One day his friends in the Marx Circle at City College informed him that a charismatic speaker at the Educational Alliance, a nearby settlement house, was denouncing socialism in a defense of individualism. Cohen and his associates decided, on a lark really, to go hear the speaker, and if possible, to disrupt his lectures. Cohen explained:

> Completely convinced of my own premises, I took advantage of the question period following the lecture to heckle the speaker, which I continued to do in later lectures, on all possible and many impossible occasions. To my surprise Davidson did not resent my views or my manners but responded to my attacks in the friendliest way.[3]

Impressed with Cohen, Davidson took him under his wing. On the pretext of needing someone to chop wood at his Glenmore Summer School of the Culture Sciences, Davidson financed Cohen's travel to his unusual school on Mt. Hurricane in the Adirondack Mountains of northeastern New York. At Glenmore, Davidson instructed Cohen and many of his young friends in world history, philosophy, and literature. Quite the taskmaster, Davidson demanded that they read primary texts in the original language. They were also permitted to attend lectures by some of the most prominent intellectuals of the day, including William Torrey Harris, editor of the *JSP;* John Dewey, then a young philosophy professor at the University of Michigan; and William James, an established philosophy professor at Harvard.

Davidson's work with Russian immigrants like Cohen was an expression of the conception of philosophy he shared with his friends in

St. Louis, according to which philosophy could serve as an antidote to suicide because it gave meaning to life. And in this regard, the philosophy expressed by the very act of publication of the *JSP* was significantly different from the philosophy of the founders of the *Philosophical Review* and the *Journal of Philosophy, Psychology, and Scientific Methods.* After a brief introduction to the chief St. Louis Hegelians, I shall focus on their conception of philosophy.

The St. Louis Hegelians

By the time Davidson, a Scottish immigrant, joined the St. Louis Hegelians in 1868, they had already coalesced into a coherent cluster of intellectuals. The group traced its beginning to Harris's chance encounter with an eccentric Pomeranian immigrant by the name of Henry Conrad Brokmeyer at the St. Louis Mercantile Library in 1858. Brokmeyer had become a proponent of Hegel's philosophy, strangely enough, after he left Prussia at the age of sixteen. Working at a series of odd jobs, Brokmeyer made his way to Memphis, Tennessee, where he operated a successful tanning, currying, and shoemaking business; he saved enough money to enter the preparatory department of Georgetown College, Kentucky, in 1850. After two years of study, Brokmeyer was threatened with expulsion because of a theological dispute with the president and traveled east to attend Brown University for two years, engaging in frequent debate with President Francis Wayland. At Brown, Brokmeyer perused Frederic Henry Hedge's *Prose Writers of Germany,* an anthology of translations of works by Kant, Fichte, Schelling, and Hegel, among others, and determined that Hegel was the greatest philosopher of all time.

Leaving Brown in 1854, Brokmeyer traveled west and took up residence in an abandoned cabin in Warren County, Missouri. Given to periods of seclusion from society under the influence of Henry David Thoreau, Brokmeyer studied philosophy in his cabin for two years. He then took a job in a St. Louis foundry, but continued to devote his evenings to philosophy, encountering Harris at a meeting of the St. Louis Philosophical and Literary Society. Harris, who had dropped out of Yale after two and a half years (1854-57) because he was dissatisfied with its predictable orthodoxy founded upon Scottish Common Sense Realism, was impressed by his new friend's knowledge of German philosophy. Succumbing to Harris's entreaties, Brokmeyer reluctantly agreed to tutor Harris and a few others, but he soon escaped to the solitary life in Warren County. Months later, Harris discovered Brokmeyer near death from "an attack of bilious fever," brought him back to St. Louis, nursed him to health, and joined with some friends to commission Brokmeyer to translate Hegel's *Science of Logic* into English.[4] Thus began Harris's lifelong efforts to "make Hegel talk English."[5] But Harris's plans were disrupted once more in 1861, this time by the outbreak of the hostilities that thrust Missouri into the bloodiest guerilla combat of the Civil War.

Originally from Connecticut, Harris was a staunch Unionist. Due to a childhood eye injury, he remained in St. Louis during the war, working as a schoolteacher and administrator and translating Hegel's *Philosophy of History,* which helped him formulate a philosophical interpretation of the war. The war plunged Brokmeyer into a philosophical struggle in which he sought to reconcile his Thoreauean sense of personal liberty with his Hegelian sense of social obligation. Like most German-Americans, he ultimately committed himself to the Union cause because he abhorred slavery and detested slave owners' claim to a right of secession from the Union.[6] Organizing a regiment, Brokmeyer served one year in the state militia before he was imprisoned for disloyalty. But in the political tumult of the times, six weeks later he was elected to the state legislature, where he served two years as a "War Democrat."

Harris and Brokmeyer concluded that the violent conflict was the result of a peculiar American philosophy of "brittle individualism." In order to counter that philosophy, after the war Harris organized the St. Louis Philosophical Society, which held its first meeting in January 1866 with Brokmeyer as president. Harris also devoted himself to his work in public education, serving as superintendent of the St. Louis public schools from 1868 to 1880 and becoming the first United States commissioner of education in 1889.

Brokmeyer opened a law practice after the war and continued to pursue his political career. He was elected to the Board of Aldermen of St. Louis in 1866. Four years later he was elected to the state senate, and, in 1875 as a member of the constitutional convention, he took a leading part in shaping the state's constitution. He ultimately rose to the position of lieutenant governor, and in 1876-77, acting governor during Governor John Smith Phelps's illness. Though Brokmeyer's disdain for the grammatical and spelling conventions of the English language doomed to failure all efforts to publish his translation of Hegel's *Logic*, his mind was crucial to the coterie of writers, educators, and professional men and women who comprised "the St. Louis Movement."[7] According to Harris,

> [Brokmeyer] could flash into the questions of the day, or even into the questions of the moment, the highest insight of philosophy and solve their problems. Even the hunting of wild turkeys or squirrels was the occasion for the use of philosophy. Philosophy came to mean with us, therefore, the most practical of all species of knowledge. We used it to solve all problems concerned with school teaching and school management. We studied the "dialectic" of politics and political parties and understood how measures and men may be combined by its light.[8]

Denton Snider, the self-appointed historian of the group, is one of the most interesting founding members of the postwar Philosophical Society. Upon graduating from Oberlin College in 1862, Snider had enlisted in the Union Army, where he rose to the rank of second lieutenant before resigning after one year because of ill health. In March 1864, he began to teach Greek and Latin in the College of the Christian Brothers in St. Louis, where he soon fell in with Harris and Brokmeyer and devoted himself to a six-year study of Hegel. A neophyte philosopher at the time, in the fall of 1866 he joined Brokmeyer's law office, ostensibly to study law, but in reality to become "a pupil of the University Brokmeyer in person."[9] Conversant in five foreign languages—Greek, Latin, French, German, and Italian—as well as the classic texts of the Western literary tradition, Snider's scholarship expanded the intellectual interests of the group beyond the confines of German philosophy.

These three men are generally described as the core of the group, but it is important to note that, according to Snider, a woman, Susan Blow, was one of the four major figures.[10] While Hegel showed little respect for women's intellectual abilities, the St. Louis Hegelians sought to curb elitist elements in his thought and, certainly in their attitudes toward women, they were more egalitarian than the German philosopher.[11] One of the few St. Louis natives of the group, Blow was the daughter of a prominent businessman and state politician. She drew upon the writings of Hegel and Friedrich Froebel to articulate a sophisticated philosophy of education that she also put into action. In 1873, she and Harris organized the first successful public kindergarten program in the United States as well as a normal school in 1874. Under Blow's leadership, the kindergarten movement grew rapidly, leading to the formation of the New York Kindergarten Association and an International Union.

Many other local professionals joined these four leaders of the group, remarkably few of whom were German-American, despite the fact that the city was crowded with German immigrants. Not all of the members of the society were followers of Hegel. Davidson obstinately argued for the superiority of Aristotle to Hegel, and Adolph Kroeger consistently preferred Kant and Fichte to Hegel. George Holmes Howison, who later built the philosophy department at the University of California–Berkeley, was always dubious of Hegel's ability to account for the reality of the individual and thus drew upon Aristotle and Leibniz to develop his own version of the philosophy of personal idealism that was fairly widespread in British and American circles by the turn of the century. Despite these differences, we can speak of a St. Louis philosophy of education, centered on the German notion of *Bildung*, which formed the core of the group's conception of philosophy.

The Lost *Bildung* Tradition in American Philosophy

In recent years, Richard Rorty has admonished philosophers to abandon epistemology-centered philosophy in favor of edifying philosophy. Rorty pointed to Hans-Georg Gadamer's hermeneutics as an example, claiming that Gadamer accomplished the shift to edifying philosophy "by substituting the notion of *Bildung* (education, self-formation) for that of 'knowledge' as the goal of thinking." Rorty explained that he preferred the notion of edification to *Bildung* because the latter sounds "a bit too foreign." But unbeknownst to Rorty (and others), there is a significant *Bildung* tradition in American philosophy that originated in St. Louis.[12] Rorty mistakenly assumed that Gadamer sought to use the notion of *Bildung* to displace Hegel's alleged pretense to provide a transcript of reality with a more modest conception of philosophy.[13] The St. Louis Hegelians' conception of *Bildung* was grounded in their study of a German humanist tradition that included the writings of Herder, Goethe, Schiller, Fichte, Schelling, Novalis, and Hegel.[14] Because the St. Louis Hegelians studied Hegel in this cultural context, their reading of his thought is at odds with Rorty's.

The St. Louis Hegelians understood the extent to which the French Revolution, which began when Hegel was nineteen years old, profoundly shaped the trajectory of his intellectual development. Though Hegel viewed the Reign of Terror as a terrible diversion from the lofty goals of the Revolution, he never abandoned his commitment to its principles of individual liberty and cosmopolitanism.[15] Revolution turned to Terror, Hegel believed, because French culture lacked liberal traditions, and the French people had not experienced the moral renewal that was necessary to true political reform. This moral renewal would come through a particular type of education, that is, through *Bildung.*[16] Only a people of *Bildung* could form a social fabric in which the social and political institutions adequate to the principles of the Revolution could be established and sustained. In addition to well-formed institutions, Hegel believed that a stable, progressive society required its own art and civic religion to help individual members internalize the society's common moral values. Unlike Robespierre's Festival of the Supreme Being of 1794, however, Hegel's civic religion had to be grounded in longstanding traditions.

In his writings on education, Hegel averred that moral instruction must be given gradually and indirectly, primarily through the study of what we now call the liberal arts.[17] With the help and support of his close friend Friedrich Immanuel Niethammer, Hegel sought to put this model of education into practice as rector of the Nuremburg *Gymnasium* from 1808 to 1815.[18] In Nuremburg, Hegel developed a philosophy of education that was opposed to past German models and the Enlightenment model of education, the latter of which he identified as "utilitarian."

Hegel's conception of *Bildung* meant that the fundamental aim of education was to place students in a position in which they could pursue a certain ideal of humanity, namely, that of becoming a self-directed, self-formed man of cultivation and taste.[19] *Bildung,* Hegel argued, involved the estrangement of the mind from its natural state through a study of art, ancient languages, and the classics, followed by a return, or reconciliation, to its own culture, language, and symbols. Through self-alienation, Hegel claimed, one rises above one's own natural inclinations and discovers universal norms of conduct. This process would afford a deeper appreciation of the universal moral principles at the core of the individual's culture and thereby promote one's sense of unity with that culture. Such an education would also take the individual beyond his local community because it was ultimately aimed at the development of a general model of humanity. Like other German humanists, Hegel sought to promote a unified German culture that was consistent with cosmopolitanism because it did not in any way imply a single national German state. He rejected the efforts of those, like his older contemporary Fichte, who sought to transform cultural nationalism into a movement for political unification. Hegel's emphatically cosmopolitan outlook led him to oppose, and even ridicule, efforts to promote German political unification.[20]

Hegel also believed *Bildung* was a precondition to independent, philosophical thought. Hence the infamous Preface to Hegel's *Phenomenology of Spirit,* the preface to his system of thought, centered on a discussion of *Bildung.* The *Phenomenology* can be profitably viewed as the story of both spirit's and the individual's *Bildung,* the goal of which is the development of the higher humanity within ourselves, which emerges as we strengthen our truly human powers and subjugate the inhuman as we strive to become complete human beings. Like Goethe's *Wilhelm Meisters Lehrjahre* and Friedrich Schiller's *Wilhelm Tell,* Hegel's *Phenomenology* is, on this reading, a *Bildungsroman,* in which the reader is shown the development of an open and intelligent mind in a complex society that lacks universally accepted values. The center of interest in a *Bildungsroman* is not the protagonist's character, adventures, or accomplishments, but the links between his successive experiences and his gradual achievement of a fully rounded personality and well-tested philosophy of life.[21]

Hegel never abandoned the notion of *Bildung;* indeed, it is a central motif in his 1821 *Philosophy of Right,* in which he illuminated the concept by repeating the advice of a Pythagorean philosopher to a father about the best way to educate his son: "Make him the *citizen of a state with good laws.*"[22] Thus the *Philosophy of Right* highlights the political connotations of *Bildung. Bildung* requires a well-ordered society in which the individual has the freedom, and even luxury, to develop his unique talents and abilities. *Bildung* also requires a society in which there is scope for all kinds of complementary individuals and activities because exposure to different kinds of people and experimentation with different types of lives is crucial to the sort of moral development Hegel had in mind. Hegel made it apparent throughout the *Philosophy of Right* that *Bildung* should begin in the family, continue more systematically in school, and be taken to a higher level in the university. After formal schooling is completed, in civil society the individual should achieve the final stage of *Bildung,* recognition of the rational basis of his society's institutions. In contrast to those who have portrayed Hegel's political thought as reactionary, the cultural and political connotations of his concept of *Bildung* were liberal in the early nineteenth-century German context. The final stage of *Bildung* does not require acquiescence to the status quo. On the contrary, the man of *Bildung* is capable of independent thought and is thus exceptionally well prepared to engage in immanent critique of his society's practices. That is to say, he is able to criticize his society on its own terms, to appraise the extent to which it measures up to its rational basis, its highest ideals.[23] Yet because Hegel believed true political reform had to be preceded by gradual cultural reform, he was never a radical. He rejected the revolutionary notion that society could be rapidly transformed.

On the epistemological level Hegel's concept of *Bildung* entails that knowledge is gained only from experience and from the widest variety of experience. This is where the humanist reading of Hegel is most clearly at odds with Rorty's, who uncritically accepts the common caricature of Hegel as one who had a disdain for experience and engaged in ungrounded metaphysical speculation.[24] Furthermore, on the *Bildung* model, learning involves activity. Hence Hegel rejected Locke's passive spectator theory of the mind, according to which we should restrain our passions in order to gain objective knowledge. For Hegel, learning requires a passionate search for truth. Hegel's notion of *Bildung* emphasized *Selbsttätigkeit,* self-activity, self-development, and self-direction. For Hegel, true education was a matter of conscious self-development that required arduous individual effort and responsibility. Yet Hegel was also critical of the "beautiful soul," the person who is so consumed with his own salvation that he has no adequate sense of the suffering in the world and is unwilling to act to counter it for fear that he will corrupt his own soul. For Hegel, fulfillment must come in the activities of real life. This point illuminates Brokmeyer's struggle to reconcile Thoreau's teachings with Hegel's. Finally, Hegel was critical of the Enlightenment's fixation on a narrow conception of knowledge, as is Rorty, arguing that *Bildung* requires self-knowledge, an accurate perception of one's talents and abilities.

Seven years after Hegel's death in 1831, one of his most important students, Karl Rosenkranz, discovered an unfinished manuscript by Hegel on education. Hegel had worked on the text during his years in Nuremburg. Rosenkranz attempted to impose some order on the patchy text and published it as a volume of Hegel's collected works under the title *Philosophische Propädeutik.* Some thirty years later, the St. Louis Hegelians began a correspondence with Rosenkranz, who probably recommended the text to them as educators. Harris translated about two-thirds of the text into English and published significant portions of it in the *JSP*. From this, and other clues, we know that the St. Louis Hegelians were well versed in Hegel's philosophy of education and understood its political implications.[25] In fact, I have argued elsewhere that during and after the Civil War, the St. Louis Hegelians engaged in precisely the sort of immanent critique of their society that Hegel espoused.[26]

During the Civil War, Harris and Brokmeyer had come to believe that the conflict was properly understood much the same way that Hegel understood the French Revolution. Sectional tensions had come to a head, they believed, because abolitionists and slave owners both appealed to the abstract, transcendent rights of the individual. Both groups conceived of the individual as existing over and against society. Abolitionists had argued that slaves had an inalienable right to freedom; Southerners defended slave ownership on the grounds that their property rights were sacred and inviolable. In Hegelian terms, both parties asserted merely formal morality, thus indicating that American *Sittlichkeit,* or concrete morality, was inadequate to the issue at hand. There was no common sense of morality adequate to the resolution of the conflict between abolitionists and slave owners. Ultimately, Snider was also convinced of this analysis of the war, and he developed it at length in several books.[27] Harris's and Snider's activities in public education after the war, and Brokmeyer's involvement in politics, were efforts to promote the formation of a progressive American *Sittlichkeit* in which moral and political disputes could be resolved without violence. The St. Louis Hegelians' *JSP* was a key part of their efforts to reform society. Though the *JSP* is often characterized as the first journal in the English language devoted to philosophy, it was in fact equally devoted to the study of art and religion because the St. Louis Hegelians believed those subjects were the paths to *Bildung* and the formation of *Sittlichkeit.*

When we place the *JSP* in the context of this philosophical project, we see why it is so different from those that followed. Cohen was correct to note that it was more concerned with religion than the *Philosophical Review* and the *Journal of Philosophy, Psychology, and Scientific Methods.* Yet it is misleading to characterize it as exemplifying a "theological" period of modern American philosophy.[28] Rather, the *JSP* was one tool, among many, of a philosophy of cultural reform. As a motto for the journal, Harris chose a passage from Novalis: "Philosophy can bake no bread, but she can procure for us God, Freedom, and Immortality." Although this quote may seem to denigrate the practicality of philosophy, Harris intended it as a declaration of what philosophy can accomplish in our lives. The *JSP* sought to promote the formation of a "true 'American' type of speculative philosophy" by providing translations of the works of ancient and modern philosophers of the Western tradition, as well as original articles on literary and art criticism, religion, science and philosophy.[29] In this way, Harris explained, the *JSP* did not break with tradition altogether. Rather it promoted the adaptation of the rational basis, the highest ideals, of the Western tradition to American soil.[30] Although the St. Louis Hegelians may not have transformed American society, the *JSP* was a great success because it provided a venue in which an important American philosophical tradition began to develop. Moreover, the *JSP* carried articles by several prominent European philosophers and was widely read in Europe, even sparking several debates that spilled over into European philosophical journals.[31]

Although it was vigorously promoted in the *JSP*, the American *Bildung* tradition has been lost because it required its proponents to be involved in the world as much as in scholarly study. As intellectuals retreated into research universities throughout the twentieth century, the philosophers of the *Bildung* tradition seemed amateurish precisely because of their social and political involvement. Hence we would do well to reflect upon the "amateur" label that has been foisted upon the St. Louis Hegelians.[32] It is unclear what the label means given the fact that the St. Louis Hegelians lived and worked, to a great extent, before higher education in the United States had become professionalized. Moreover, as superintendent of the St. Louis public schools and as United States commissioner of education, Harris promoted the professionalization of public education.

Does the label "amateur" mean that the St. Louis Hegelians were less scholarly than contemporary academic philosophers? In a day when philosophers can obtain tenure at most universities with less than a half-dozen articles published and no books, it is difficult to see how the most important St. Louis Hegelians could have been less qualified than current "professionals."[33] Snider published more than fifty books, and a bibliography of Harris's publications comprises thirty-five pages.[34] Moreover, the St. Louis Hegelians' philological work manifests an intensity of scholarship unequaled in the American academy since the late nineteenth century. One scholar has estimated that Davidson knew thirteen languages by the time of his death; in addition to ancient Latin and Greek, as well as modern French and German, Davidson's languages included Sanskrit, Icelandic, and Arabic.[35] We have noted that Snider knew five languages and should add that he studied Hegel's complete works in the German edition edited by Leopold Von Henning.

"Professional" might also connote the secularization of intellectuals that Cohen alluded to. But secularization of American intellectual life has occurred by degrees. As Henry Pochmann notes,

> The men of St. Louis were distinguished more for their aloofness from churches than for their adherence to religious creeds. Emerson, when he first met the group, half jocularly but approvingly spoke of Harris and his "German atheists." They neither were nor became apostles of any form of religious dogma or theological doctrine; but they were, to a man, profoundly religious and thoughtful—intent upon nothing less than the

> solution of the fundamental problems of man. They were philosophers of the kind whose philosophy impinges at every point on religion.[36]

If by "professional" we mean a scholar who specializes narrowly and addresses her colleagues almost exclusively in her work, then the St. Louis Hegelians would reject the label on sophisticated philosophical grounds. Rather than "amateurs," I prefer to describe the St. Louis Hegelians as "proto-professional" philosophers because they initiated the move toward professionalization of philosophy by self-consciously promoting a degree of scholarly rigor that many of the New England Transcendentalists lacked. The notion that the St. Louis Hegelians were "amateur" philosophers is based on an anachronistic standard that blurs their conception of philosophy as *Bildung*.[37]

Davidson's work in New York City and at Glenmore provides a splendid, concrete example of what the St. Louis Hegelians hoped to accomplish. Wintering in New York City, Davidson devoted his time to reaching young immigrants like Cohen. Each summer, for the last ten years of his life, Davidson took groups of these young men and women to Glenmore, in effect, alienating them from ghetto life, and gave them a vision, in the scenic beauty of Mt. Hurricane, of what society could be through study of the great works of the Western tradition. When these young men and women returned to their homes in the ghetto at the end of the summer, they had been utterly transformed, and many of them went on to lead various reform movements of the Progressive Era. Elizabeth Flower and Murray Murphey correctly note that Davidson's "[s]tudents grew into professionals and teachers, and the list of those associated with the college reads like a *Who's Who* of the next generation's intelligentsia and reformers."[38]

Shortly after Davidson's death in 1900, however, American philosophy changed in ways that obscured the American *Bildung* tradition. After the founding of the American Philosophical Association in 1901, American philosophy focused on issues much more narrowly conceived than the meaning of life. Despite important exceptions, philosophers in America no longer viewed philosophy as an antidote to suicide. The philosophers who were exceptions to this trend, for example, Morris Cohen and John Dewey, were old enough to have been profoundly influenced by the St. Louis Hegelians. Study of the St. Louis Hegelians can provide us with deeper understanding of this transformation of American philosophy, as well as ways to conceptualize philosophy, once again, as a fundamentally practical activity.

NOTES

1. Morris R. Cohen, "The Conception of Philosophy in Recent Discussion," *The Journal of Philosophy, Psychology, and Scientific Methods* 7, no. 5 (July 21, 1910): 401.

2. For biographical information on Cohen, see Morris R. Cohen, *A Dreamer's Journey: The Autobiography of Morris Raphael Cohen* (Boston: Beacon Press, 1949); Leonora Rosenfield Cohen, *Portrait of a Philosopher: Morris R. Cohen in Life and Letters* (New York: Harcourt, Brace, and World, 1962); and David A. Hollinger, *Morris Cohen and the Scientific Ideal* (Cambridge: MIT Press, 1975).

3. Cohen, *A Dreamer's Journey,* 103.

4. William Schuyler, "German Philosophy in St. Louis," *The Bulletin of the Washington University Association,* no. 2 (April 23, 1904): 68.

5. Denton Snider, *The St. Louis Movement in Philosophy, Literature, Education, Psychology, with Chapters of Autobiography* (St. Louis: Sigma Publishing Company, 1920), 279. Cf. William H. Goetzmann, ed., *The American Hegelians: An Intellectual Episode in the History of Western America* (New York: Alfred A. Knopf, 1973), 3; and Dorothy Rogers, "'Making Hegel Talk English': America's First Women Idealists," Ph.D. diss., Boston University, 1998.

6. James A. Good, "A 'World-Historical Idea': The St. Louis Hegelians and the Civil War," *Journal of American Studies* 34, no. 1 (December 2000): 447-64; James A. Good, *A Search for Unity in Diversity: The "Permanent Hegelian Deposit" in the Philosophy of John Dewey* (Lanham, Md.: Lexington Books, 2006), 66-70.

7. Many of the St. Louis Hegelians commented on Brokmeyer's contempt for the English language; he even varied the way he spelled his name. Snider notes that Brokmeyer's translation of Hegel's *Logic* "needed revision in the matter of orthography, of syntax, of general style" (Snider, *A Writer of Books in His Genesis; Written for and Dedicated to His Pupil-friends Reaching Back in a Line of Fifty Years* [St. Louis: Sigma Publishing Co., 1910], 318, cf. 324-25).

8. W. T. Harris, *Hegel's Logic: A Book on the Genesis of the Categories of the Mind* (Chicago: S. C. Griggs, 1890), xiii. On the St. Louis Hegelians' commitment to philosophy as a practical endeavor see also Snider, *A Writer of Books,* 317.

9. Snider, *The St. Louis Movement*, 11.

10. Ibid., 301.

11. Although no women are listed in the membership rolls of the St. Louis Philosophical Society, Harris, Snider, Davidson, and others were leaders in local efforts to obtain suffrage for women. Furthermore, as superintendent of the St. Louis public schools,

Harris treated women employees exceptionally well. Stephen L. McIntyre, "'Our Schools are Not Charitable Institutions': Class, Gender, Ethnicity, and the Teaching Profession in Nineteenth-Century St. Louis," *Missouri Historical Review* 92 (October 1997): 27-44. The best source on the women of the group is Rogers, "'Making Hegel Talk English.'" For membership in the society, see Kurt Leidecker, ed., *The Record Book of the St. Louis Philosophical Society Founded February 1866* (Lewiston, N.Y.: The Edwin Mellen Press, 1990). On the St. Louis Hegelians' effort to Americanize Hegel by assuaging his elitism, see Frances B. Harmon, *The Social Philosophy of the St. Louis Hegelians* (New York: Columbia University, 1943), esp. 97-105. Cf. Mary Forrest Dowling, "The St. Louis Movement: Reconstruction of the Individual and the Nation through Speculative Philosophy," Ph.D. diss., St. Louis University, 1972, 123-31. On Hegel's sexism, see Terry Pinkard, *Hegel: A Biography* (Cambridge: Cambridge University Press, 2000), 288ff; and Lewis P. Hinchman, *Hegel's Critique of the Enlightenment* (Gainesville and Tampa: The University Presses of Florida, 1984), 104ff.

12. Richard Rorty, *Philosophy and the Mirror of Nature* (Princeton: Princeton University Press, 1979), 359, 360. The following is a development of the discussion of Hegel's and the St. Louis Hegelians' concepts of *Bildung* in Michael H. DeArmey and James A. Good, "Introduction," *Cultural, National, and World Unity,* vol. 2 of *The St. Louis Hegelians* (Bristol, Eng.: Thoemmes Press, 2001), vii-viii.

13. Though Gadamer is certainly critical of Hegel, he self-consciously drew upon Hegel's development of the notion of *Bildung.* Hans-Georg Gadamer, *Truth and Method,* 2d rev. ed. (New York: The Crossroad Publishing Corporation, 1989), 12.

14. For an outstanding study of the humanist tradition I have in mind, see W. H. Bruford, *The German Tradition of Self-Cultivation: "Bildung" from Humboldt to Thomas Mann* (Cambridge: Cambridge University Press, 1975).

15. Many authors have documented Hegel's lifelong commitment to the principles of the Revolution. An important source on this topic is Joachim Ritter, *Hegel and the French Revolution: Essays on the Philosophy of Right,* trans. Richard Dien Winfield (Cambridge: The MIT Press, 1982).

16. In the following discussion of Hegel's concept of *Bildung,* I am indebted to John H. Smith, *The Spirit and Its Letter: Traces of Rhetoric in Hegel's Philosophy of "Bildung"* (Ithaca: Cornell University Press, 1988).

17. Hegel, *The Philosophical Propadeutic,* trans. A. V. Miller, ed. Michael George and Andrew Vincent (Oxford: Basil Blackwell, 1986).

18. In 1808, Niethammer was appointed to a high governmental position in Munich, *Zentralschul und Oberkirchenrat,* central commissioner of education and Consistory, and immediately set to work reforming Bavarian education. Niethammer appointed Hegel to his position in Nuremburg to help an old friend, but also because the two agreed on the *Bildung* model of education. Terry Pinkard groups Niethammer, and by implication Hegel, in the "neo-humanist" tradition along with Wilhelm von Humboldt. Pinkard, *Hegel,* 269ff.

19. In my discussion of Hegel's thought I have used gender specific language precisely because he believed only men were capable of the sort of intellectual development he championed.

20. Though Hegel's cosmopolitanism led him to oppose political unification of the German states, it also made him critical of their excessive localism. These are prominent themes in Pinkard, *Hegel.*

21. Josiah Royce is generally credited with being the first English-speaking scholar to articulate this reading of the *Phenomenology* in his *Lectures on Modern Idealism* (1919). James Livingston has recently shown that Jean Wahl and Alexandre Kojève, key figures in the twentieth-century renaissance of the humanistic reading of Hegel, were both influenced by Royce's efforts to displace the sort of metaphysical reading whose truth Rorty seems to assume. Livingston, *Pragmatism, Feminism, and Democracy: Rethinking the Politics of American History* (New York: Routledge, 2001), 61-64. Yet no one has considered the extent to which the St. Louis Hegelians' humanistic Hegelianism influenced Royce. Royce published his first article in the *JSP* (see below), and since it was the only philosophical journal available for many years, it is safe to assume that Royce studied its pages. Moreover, Royce was a frequent lecturer at Davidson's Glenmore Summer School of the Culture Sciences during the 1890s.

22. Hegel, *Elements of the Philosophy of Right,* trans. H. B. Nisbet, ed. Allen W. Wood (Cambridge: Cambridge University Press, 1991), §153 (emphasis in the original). Hegel also quoted this advice in his *Natural Law* essay, written in late 1802, early 1803. Hegel, *Natural Law: The Scientific Ways of Treating Natural Law, Its Place in Moral Philosophy, and Its Relation to the Positive Sciences of Law,* trans. T. M. Knox (Philadelphia: University of Pennsylvania Press, 1975), 115.

23. According to Steven B. Smith, Hegel was "the great champion of . . . immanent critique." On Smith's reading, cultural criticism is the primary purpose of Hegel's dialectic. Smith, *Hegel's Critique of Liberalism: Rights in Context* (Chicago: The University of Chicago Press, 1989), 10.

24. Among other places, Rorty's perception of Hegel is apparent in his response to Allen Hance's insightful essay in Herman J. Saatkamp, Jr., ed., *Rorty and Pragmatism: The Philosopher Responds to His Critics* (Nashville: Vanderbilt University Press, 1995), 122-25.

25. The St. Louis Hegelians also studied Rosenkranz's *Pädagogik als System,* which was translated by Anna Brackett, another important woman of the St. Louis group. All totaled, well over one hundred pages of the *JSP* were devoted to translations of Rosenkranz's commentary on Hegel. On the importance of Rosenkranz's "center Hegelianism" and its influence on the St. Louis Hegelians, see Michael H. DeArmey and James A. Good, "Introduction," *Origins, the Dialectic and the Critique of Materialism,* vol. 1 of *The St. Louis Hegelians* (Bristol, Eng.: Thoemmes Press, 2001), xvii-xviii.

26. Good, "A 'World-Historical Idea.'"

27. See especially Snider's works, *The American Ten Years' War, 1855-1865* (St. Louis: Sigma Publishing Co., 1906); *Abraham Lincoln, an Interpretation in Biography* (St. Louis: Sigma Publishing Co., 1908); *A Writer of Books;* and *The St. Louis Movement.*

28. In the *JSP* and elsewhere, Harris undertook a defense of the Christian doctrine of the Trinity. Yet none of the other principal St. Louis Hegelians seem to have shared Harris's concern about orthodox Christianity. According to Denton Snider, the group sought to overthrow traditional American religion in favor of one that was more

universal. "We sought to win a fresh spiritual communion with the Divine Order and its Orderer, and to create for the same a new unborn expression. But to accomplish any such purpose we had to throw aside the old carcass of tradition . . . and to begin over." Snider, *The St. Louis Movement,* 24-26.

29. Harris, *JSP* 1, no. 1 (1867): 1.

30. See Edward L. Schaub, ed., *William Torrey Harris, 1835-1935: A Collection of Essays, Including Papers and Addresses Presented in Commemoration of Dr. Harris' Centennial at the St. Louis Meeting of the Western Division of the American Philosophical Society* (Chicago and London: The Open Court Publishing Co., 1936), 21-22.

31. Both Dewey and Josiah Royce published their first article in the *JSP*. Dewey, "The Metaphysical Assumptions of Materialism," *JSP* 16 (April 1882): 208-13; Royce, "Schiller's Ethical Studies," *JSP* 12 (1878): 373-92. G. Stanley Hall published his second scholarly work in the *JSP*. Hall, "Anti-Materialism," *JSP* 6 (July 1872): 216-22. According to Dewey, Peirce first articulated "the conclusion that all thought was in signs and required a time," which led to "his pragmaticism, his theory of signs, and his search for a functional logic" in *JSP* in 1868. Dewey and Arthur Bentley, *Knowing and the Known* (1949), in vol. 16 of *The Later Works, 1925-1953,* ed. Jo Ann Boydston (Carbondale: Southern Illinois University Press, 1981-91), 238-39. Peirce's four articles are: "Questions Concerning Certain Faculties Claimed for Man," *JSP* 2 (1868): 103; "Some Consequences of Four Incapacities," *JSP* 2 (1868): 140; "On the Meaning of 'Determined,'" *JSP* 2 (1868): 190; and "Grounds of the Validity of the Laws of Logic," *JSP* 2 (1868): 193. Several important European intellectuals, like Rosenkranz, were auxiliary members of the St. Louis Philosophical Society, specifically James Hutchinson Stirling, Ludwig Feuerbach, and J. H. Fichte, among others. One example of a debate that carried over into European journals concerned the issue of whether or not Hegel's philosophy was pantheistic or theistic. See Franz Hoffman, "The Hegelian Philosophy in St. Louis in the United States of North America" in DeArmey and Good, eds., *Origins, the Dialectic and the Critique of Materialism,* 92-96. Hoffman's article originally appeared in the *Philosophische Monatshefte* in 1871.

32. Elizabeth Flower and Murray G. Murphey, *A History of Philosophy in America*, vol. 2 (New York: Putnam, 1976), 505; Bruce Kuklick, *Churchmen and Philosophers: From Jonathan Edwards to John Dewey* (New Haven: Yale University Press, 1985), 183.

33. These numbers are based on my conversations with philosophy professors at meetings of the American Philosophical Association and elsewhere.

34. Henry R. Evans, ed., "A List of the Writings of William Torrey Harris," *Report of the Commissioner of Education for 1907* (Washington, D.C.: Government Printing Office, 1908): 37-72; Arthur E. Bostwick, "List of Books Written by Denton J. Snider, Litt. D., with Annotations," *St. Louis Public Library Monthly Bulletin* (August 1924), 1-8.

35. Michael H. DeArmey, "Thomas Davidson's Apeirotheism and its Influence on William James and John Dewey," *Journal of the History of Ideas* 48 (Oct.-Dec.), 691-708.

36. Henry Pochmann, *New England Transcendentalism and St. Louis Hegelianism: Phases in the History of American Idealism* (Philadelphia: Carl Schurz Memorial Foundation, 1948), 27.

37. Cf. DeArmey and Good, "Introduction," *Origins, the Dialectic and the Critique of Materialism,* xix-xx. In some ways the St. Louis Hegelians can be compared to the members of the American Social Science Association (1865-1909). Both groups differed from their twentieth-century counterparts in that they were actively involved in social reform. See Thomas Haskell, *The Emergence of Professional Social Science: The American Social Science Association and the Nineteenth-Century Crisis of Authority,* 2d ed. (Baltimore and London: The Johns Hopkins University Press, 2000). Yet Haskell refers to the members of the ASSA as "amateur" social scientists, a label I reject for the St. Louis Hegelians. On the St. Louis Hegelians' efforts to promote philosophical rigor in New England, see Pochmann, *New England Transcendentalism and St. Louis Hegelianism.*

38. Flower and Murphey, *A History of Philosophy in America,* vol. 2, 486. Snider engaged in similar work in several midwestern cities, including work with Jane Addams at Hull House. For discussions of Snider's fascinating life, see D. H. Harris, *A Brief Report of the Meeting Commemorative of the Early Saint Louis Movement in Philosophy, Psychology, Literature, Art and Education* (St. Louis: n.p., 1922).

THE ST. LOUIS HEGELIANS AND NEW ENGLAND PRAGMATISTS

Douglas R. Anderson, Southern Illinois University–Carbondale

CHARLES SANDERS PEIRCE ROUTINELY ALIGNED PERSONS WITH HIS THREE categories of firstness, secondness, and thirdness. Persons of firstness were champions of immediate perception and poetry; persons of secondness were practically oriented and aimed to get things done; and persons of thirdness were lovers of theory, whose chief aim is to pursue the truth. This categorial sketch is useful for thinking about how Hegel's philosophy was appropriated by the three prominent American pragmatists: Peirce himself, William James, and John Dewey. All three, insofar as they were philosophers, were theoretically oriented; nevertheless, within that framework we can exercise Peirce's categorial distinctions as a way of tracing the philosophical emphases of each thinker.

James read Hegel seriously as early as 1867, and he remained throughout his career the most explicitly anti-Hegelian of the pragmatists. James distrusted what he considered the unnecessary complexity and necessity attached to Hegel's systematic outlook. "His system," James said, "resembles a mouse-trap, in which if you once pass the door you may be lost forever."[1] Despite such outright dismissals of Hegel's larger project, James was not oblivious to some of its virtues. Indeed, after re-examining Hegel while under the influence of nitrous oxide, James wrote that he came to believe "with unutterable power of conviction that Hegelism was true after all, and that the deepest convictions of my intellect hitherto were wrong."[2] Though this remark was offered with a bit of humor, James did see in Hegel's *Phenomenology* a working predecessor to his own radical empiricism. At his best, James argued, Hegel "plants himself in the empirical flux of things and gets the impression of what happens.

His mind is in very truth *impressionistic*."[3] Thus, James was a firstness Hegelian, appropriating the immediacy and poesy of phenomenological engagement with the world.

John Dewey, I would argue, is a secondness Hegelian. He was interested, as James Good has carefully shown, in the social efficacy of Hegelianism.[4] This put him in line with the St. Louis Movement. If one carefully reads his essays from the 1890s, such as "Reconstruction," one can see Hegel being brought into a natural social setting. Even in his later work Dewey retained an undergirding of Hegelian thought in his notions of communication, institutional reform, and transformation of nature and culture.

Peirce was by his own admission a thirdness student of Hegel; he was interested in the overall structure of the metaphysical outlook as well as in its practical consequences insofar as these, from a pragmatic point of view, helped give meaning to the system itself. Beginning in the 1860s, Peirce read Hegel's work closely and began to develop his fundamentally ambivalent attitude toward Hegel and Hegelianism. On the one hand, he believed that Hegel's insights regarding organic development and a logic of events were important and novel. On the other, he believed Hegel's limitations in logic and mathematics prevented him from developing the importance of his insights. Throughout his career, then, Peirce moved back and forth from identifying Hegel as one of the greatest thinkers to characterizing him as a novice in technical philosophy.

The point to be taken away here is that each of the pragmatists felt compelled to deal with Hegelianism. This serious philosophical engagement with Hegel's thought was not generated by their encounters with William Torrey Harris and the St. Louis Movement. However, it is unequivocally the case that the pragmatists' *development* of their engagements with Hegel was heavily influenced by their ongoing relations with members of the St. Louis Movement. All three published in the *Journal of Speculative Philosophy;* all three corresponded with Harris; and all three were brought to rethink their relations to Hegel through conversations and correspondence with Harris and others from the St. Louis community.

Leaving Dewey's story to Good's excellent treatment, I want to sketch here two stories that explore the relations among Peirce, James, and the

St. Louis Hegelians. Peirce's year-and-a-half-long correspondence with Harris and his resultant publications in the *JSP* are well known and well documented. However, three paragraphs that Harris wrote in response to Peirce's questioning of Harris's account of Paul Janet and Hegel have been overlooked. It is to these paragraphs that I will turn my attention, for it seems to me that Harris's remarks in these passages may have had a greater impact on Peirce's thinking than has heretofore been recognized.

The Jamesian story is a bit different. James's attendance at the Saturday Hegel Club run by Harris in Cambridge in the early 1880s is also well documented. Most famously, James repeatedly stated his distaste for Harris's leadership at the meetings, calling him "tedious." However, two other members of the St. Louis Movement—George Holmes Howison and Thomas Davidson—also attended these meetings and were close friends of James. My second sketch, therefore, involves the impact these two thinkers had on the way James's philosophical thought and practice developed from 1890 until his death in 1910.

Peirce and St. Louis

Peirce and Harris began their correspondence on January 1, 1868. In his initial letter Peirce offered a sop to Cerberus regarding Hegel's work: "I admit there is music in the logic of Hegel, but that is all I discover there."[5] This view he would modify over the course of his career, in part *because* of his exchanges with Harris. Later, in April of the same year, Peirce pointed out to Harris that he was "by no means thoroughly anti-transcendentalist."[6] As the year progressed, Harris continued to characterize Peirce's outlook in terms of his understanding of Hegel; Peirce was thus pushed to consider seriously his agreements and disagreements with Hegel. Also, in June of 1868 Peirce recommended to Harris an essay by a "young gentleman in the Senior class" for publication in the *JSP*. The essay Peirce described as "a statement of the historical differences between the Nominalists and the Realists," a matter, he added, "not commonly understood at all."[7] This reference was in keeping with Peirce's first contribution to the *JSP*—a portion of a letter he had written to Harris regarding Harris's essay on Paul Janet and Hegel. The piece was entitled "Nominalism vs. Realism."

In this publication Peirce began to explore the medieval distinction between two forms of logical indeterminacy: generality, in which a term can apply variously to any of a variety of particulars or concretes, and vagueness, in which a term, as he put it, "has no precise meaning." Peirce continued to develop the import of this distinction over the course of his career and used it to distinguish the categories of firstness (vagueness) and thirdness (generality) as modes of being. What I am suggesting here is that it was Harris's response to this opening publication that catalyzed Peirce's ongoing examination of the nature of reality. We know, for example, that Peirce's early *JSP* articles—the so-called "cognition" series—worked with a seminal version of Peirce's future-oriented relation between reality and truth. But I think it was as important to Peirce's later architectonic that Harris led him to dwell on the implications of nominalism.

Harris's first response to Peirce in print I take to be the source of this re-orienting of Peirce's thought. I include it here in full:

> The whole question of the validity of formal logic and of common sense vs. speculative philosophy can be reduced to this: Do you believe that there are any finite or dependent beings? In other words, are you a nominalist or a realist?
>
> *This is the gist of all philosophizing*: If one holds that things are not dependent, but that each is for itself, he will hold that general terms correspond to no object, and may get along with formal logic; and if he holds that he knows things directly in their essence, he needs no philosophy—common sense is sufficient.
>
> But if he holds that any particular thing is dependent upon what lies beyond its immediate limits, he holds, virtually, that its true being lies beyond it, or, more precisely, that its immediate being is not identical with its total being, and hence, that it is in contradiction with itself, and is therefore *changeable, transitory,* and *evanescent* regarded from the *immediate* point of view. But regarding the entire or total being (The Generic), we cannot call it changeable or contradictory, for that perpetually abides. It is the "Form of Eternity."[8]

I have room here only for a quick sketch, but my contention is that the key developments in Peirce's later architectonic can be read as a direct response to these three paragraphs. Peirce did come to argue that whether one is a nominalist or a realist is "the gist of all philosophizing." He believed something like the nominalist view in paragraph two was defended by William of Occam, such that formal logic was to be held in abeyance from dealing with matters of fact. Peirce designated Occam as the source of nominalism that, he believed, came to infest modern philosophy, especially the tradition of British empiricism. "In one word," he said, "all modern philosophy of every sect has been nominalistic."[9]

On this score, then, Peirce admitted to Harris in May of 1868, "I should come on the same side as Hegel, because I am idealistic."[10] For Peirce, idealism or transcendentalism, as Harris suggested, was a natural ally of scholastic realism insofar as it is committed to the real efficacy ideas. Peirce spent much of his later career attacking nominalism as the most dangerous philosophical disease of modern philosophy, revealing time and again its baffling consequences for science and everyday life. He was committed to the pragmatic belief that "though the question of realism and nominalism has its roots in the technicalities of logic, its branches reach about our life."[11] On the positive side, he developed and defended his own version of scholastic realism (which he called Scotistic realism) that argued for the reality of both generality and possibility—the general and the vague. There are two central implications of this realism—implications not only for the problems of philosophers but for the problems of persons. The first implication is that there is a logic of events or of the universe, not just a formal, mentalistic logic. Peirce here agreed with Hegel in principle but not in detail. As he put it in 1898: "It is true that the whole universe and every feature of it must be regarded as rational, that is as brought about by the logic of events."[12] His problem with Hegel's version of this view was that Hegel took "rational" to mean deductive; for Peirce the logic of events might "be that of the inductive or hypothetic inference."[13] The second implication is that science became intelligible as a human practice when natural laws and human habits were understood as reals. This move put Peirce clearly in the company of Hegel, Schelling, and American transcendentalism. His idealism, driven by its Scotistic realism, thus produced a philosophical kinship with the members of the St. Louis Movement.

However, Peirce also saw several important challenges in Harris's paragraphs. The first was Harris's suggestion that philosophy could be reduced to two opposing camps—the camp of speculation and the camp of common sense. For Peirce, these outlooks needed to be seen in dialectical relation. After 1868, he worked hard to develop a synthesis of German idealism and British common sensism. His central worry was not that Hegel and Harris had no sense of the concrete. Rather, it was the suggestion that the concrete in its entirety or totality could be gathered up into an unchangeable essence "that perpetually abides"—that lives in the "Forms of Eternity." As Peirce later argued, "The brute element exists and must not be explained away as Hegel seeks to do."[14]

Peirce's resistance to this feature of Harris's Hegelianism had several dimensions. First, he was sensitive to James's worry about a box universe in which everything was in principle final or finished. For him, generality did not entail necessity and closure. Thus, he developed his tychism, arguing that spontaneity or chance was an ongoing aspect of the cosmos. In short, the logic of the universe was not based on deduction, but on an abductive/inductive process that was evolutionary and whose outcome could not be predicted in concrete detail but only generally and statistically. Abduction, Peirce argued in 1903, is the logic of pragmatism. This meant that, for Peirce, even general laws and habits were open to historical modification and radical change. His adherence to the general import of Darwinian thought made his objective idealism conditional in nature. This, he saw, took him beyond Harris, and probably beyond Hegel.

A second dimension of Peirce's resistance to Harris's Hegelianism had to do with the way in which the concrete was totalized. Peirce, like James, argued that the universe of concreteness was continuous and shot through with relations. A Peircean self or personality, therefore, was never a matter of "immediate limits" but was an ongoing developmental history. Generality, as he sometimes put it, has a life or career. In this much, Peirce was a standard idealist—he was in agreement with Harris. However, as Harris seemed to suggest in this passage, the concrete, in achieving its perpetuity in the Form of Eternity, seems to leave behind its concreteness. Its particularity is taken up into the generality of the One, the Spirit. This was the very problem Josiah Royce attempted to resolve in *The World and the Individual.* The upshot of such a move, Peirce believed, was contrary to experience, contrary to the instinctive beliefs of common sense, and contrary to the basic practices of science. Hegel, he repeatedly argued, lost sight of the "outward clash" in human experience. In systematic terms, Hegel introduced the first two categories of being only to have them taken up into the third. Thus Peirce argued in 1904: "The truth is that pragmaticism is closely allied to the Hegelian absolute idealism, from which, however, it is sundered by its vigorous denial that the third category (which Hegel degrades to a mere stage of thinking) suffices to make the world, or is even so much as self-sufficient. Had Hegel, instead of regarding the first two stages with his smile of contempt, held on to them as independent or distinct elements of the triune reality, pragmaticists might have looked up to him as the great vindicator of their truth."[15]

If one pays close attention to Peirce's work in 1868-69, one can see these ideas developing in fledgling form. It would be too much to say that the working out of these ideas constituted the rest of Peirce's philosophical career, but it is appropriate to say that these ideas remained what Peirce called "leading ideas" in his subsequent work. He was quite openly a pragmatic idealist whose task was to develop a critical common sensism that took the *reality* of natural laws, statistical ranges, historical genres, and human communities seriously. The influence of Harris as catalyst in this Peircean project should not be overlooked.

James and St. Louis

James's relation to Harris was hardly as cordial as Peirce's. He sniped at Harris for not publishing a wider range of materials in the *JSP*. To his close friends, as noted, he described Harris as a "mystic" and as "tedious." Responding to Harris's Saturday Hegel Club meetings, James said, "He revolves like a squirrel in a cage in one circle of ideas; all openings presently lead into that circle and then the monstrous whirring begins."[16] Nevertheless, James routinely attended the meetings in the early 1880s. At the very least, we can say that Harris helped keep James in touch with American Hegelianism. And, as Ralph Barton Perry suggests,

> Despite this early and lasting dislike of its form James continued his study of Hegelian philosophy intermittently throughout his life, with what was on the whole an increasing respect. In the 70s and early 80s he was reading the translations and expositions of Hegel published in the *Journal of Speculative Philosophy* by W. T. Harris "our most prominent American Hegelian."[17]

Despite his less-than-agreeable interactions with Harris, James's thought was modified in both direct and subtle ways by two close friends, both of whom spent time with the Brokmeyer/Harris "school" of philosophy in St. Louis. These were the itinerant Scotsman Thomas Davidson and George Holmes Howison, who later developed the philosophy program at the University of California-Berkeley from which emerged Josiah Royce. Howison's effect on James was real, but for the most part, like that of Harris, was in a negative mode. When James wrote outlandish things about Hegel and Hegelism—which was relatively often—Howison invariably wrote to chastise him and to argue that James should rethink the particularities of his critiques. This seems innocuous enough, but if one follows the correspondence closely, one sees a genuine effect of Howison's persistence in getting James to see where his own views were still closely allied to features of idealism. We can see this in an exemplary case. James routinely defended the agency and freedom of the will, after his close readings of Renouvier's essays from mid-century. After he presented "The Dilemma of Determinism" as a talk, James received from Howison several letters detailing his concerns with James's approach. He maintained that though James's clear defense of negative freedom was praiseworthy, it was incomplete. "The thing is," he argued, "to get a view of divine nature, and of human nature, and of external nature, as to secure the foreseen inevitable along with the self-decision . . . of the individual person."[18] That is, from Howison's quasi-Hegelian idealistic outlook, James simply ignored the positive freedom that required an ontological account of what is actually possible for the will given its natural environment. The individual will must, after all, work in league with other things and other persons. Though James's initial response to Howison was flippant, he clearly noted Howison's concerns later in his career when developing his notions of continuity and relatedness, and when thinking through his final metaphysical speculations on novelty. In another instance, we see that Howison's personal idealism, unlike the similar personalism of Borden Bowne, was pluralistic—he argued, contra Royce and Bowne, for the real individuality of persons and for their independent creative powers. On this score, the exchanges between Howison and James show a clear record of mutual influence and development. Howison revealed to James an avenue by which pragmatism and idealism could be in part synthesized.

Thomas Davidson's relationship with James was more personally and philosophically intense. Davidson introduced James to his wife-to-be, Alice. Moreover, Davidson, whatever his philosophical outlook, exemplified for James the ideal of an independent, renegade scholar. Because of Davidson's abilities in communicating with young thinkers and despite his personal quirks, James tried to secure a teaching position for Davidson at Harvard. It is unlikely, however, that Davidson would have accepted had a position been offered. He routinely advised younger scholars to avoid the academy like the plague; he believed that universities imprisoned one's thought and forced one to engage in defensive philosophy rather than in the development of new thought. It is easy to see, therefore, that Davidson was at the heart of James's diatribe against the "Ph. D. Octopus" in his famous essay of that name.

In a similar vein, Davidson was a compatriot in James's championing of "popular" philosophy. The idea was not to water down philosophy to simplistic clichés. Rather, for Davidson, the aim was to "level upward"—to elevate culture as a whole; "the task of the twentieth century," he argued, is "to raise mankind, every member of it, to complete and actual moral freedom, which rests upon insight, just affection, and strong will, realizing themselves in a social order."[19] Only in this way, he suggested, would democracy have a chance of success. The St. Louis Movement, with its emphasis on everything from the advocacy of kindergarten to the enculturation of the city, was a part of Davidson's education. Harris's role as commissioner of education was directly in line with the sorts of things Davidson was suggesting in relating philosophy to culture, though Harris's Hegelianism led to a much narrower conception of learning than that of Davidson. Davidson started his own summer school in philosophy—Glenmore—in the Adirondack Mountains of New York. There he hosted Royce, James, and other scholars together with young men and women from around the country. John Dewey and his brother had land next door and also participated in many of the discussions. The idea was to provide a general schooling in culture in a non-university setting. Later, Davidson created what he called the "Breadwinners' College" in New York City. His aim was to provide a liberal education for young laborers, many of Jewish descent, after working hours. Though Davidson died not long after the school opened, his protégé, Morris Cohen, took it over and ran it successfully for a number of years, producing an important cohort of New York intellectuals, among them Herbert Schneider, the well-known historian of American philosophy.

Because of his work with Chautauqua and his emphasis on popular philosophy, James is often thought of as a philosopher of the people. But his letters—especially his early letters—reveal a young man with decidedly aristocratic inclinations. Early on James ridiculed and discounted the abilities of the working class. Indeed, his own privilege blinded him to the plight of Irish immigrants in New England. Given this, it would be a mistake not to acknowledge the impact that Davidson's ideas, conversations, commitments, and sheer force of character had on James's approach to philosophy and on his approach to the writing of philosophy.

Regarding the content of James's thought, it is more difficult to get a read on Davidson's influence. In light of James's letters and notes, it seems that much of Davidson's direct philosophical influence occurred in their personal conversations. These conversations were numerous and extensive. Davidson was more inspired by Aristotle and Rosmini than by Hegel. His written works tended toward the scholarly except when he was writing about education and culture. Nevertheless, as with Howison, two features of Davidson's outlook square with James's vision: his individualism and his pluralism.

Davidson understood the need for meliorism and for natural and cultural contexts in which individual freedom could flourish. But beyond establishing the necessary conditions for a positive freedom, Davidson, like James, championed the individual will in the transformation of self and culture. In Davidson's view this meant jettisoning reliance on some all-powerful God: "When we have done away with God," he argued, "and shifted the responsibility for the well-being of the world upon our shoulders where it belongs, we shall begin to feel the duties of consciousness to the universe."[20] For him, as for James, the future at any given time is "up to us."

Like Howison, Davidson could also be called, as Perry points out, a "pluralistic idealist." However, Davidson's pluralism seemed to have a harder edge than Howison's, an edge that would have appealed to James. In rejecting God, Davidson rejected any all-encompassing ONE:

"Existence," he argued, "is an infinite multiplicity of feelings capable of modifying each other and becoming objects to each other."[21] Compare this to what James later wrote in 1905 in "The Thing and Its Relations": "Pure experience in this state is but another name for feeling or sensation."[22] As this experience becomes fluid, James says, we find that

> the continuities and the discontinuities are absolutely co-ordinate matters of immediate feeling. The conjunctions are as primordial elements of "fact" as are the distinctions and disjunctions. In the same act by which I feel that this passing minute is a new pulse of my life, I feel that the old life continues into it, and the feeling of continuance in no wise jars upon the simultaneous feeling of novelty. They, too, compenetrate harmoniously. Prepositions, copulas, and conjunctions, "is," "isn't," "then," "before," "in," "on," "beside," "between," "next," "like," "unlike," "as," "but," flower out of the stream of pure experience, the stream of concretes or the sensational stream, as naturally as nouns and adjectives do, and they melt into it again as fluidly when we apply them to a new portion of the stream.[23]

The depth of influence seems apparent.

My aim in telling these stories of philosophical interbreeding is not simply to champion the importance of Hegel or idealism in pragmatic thought, though I do believe this connection is routinely ignored. Rather, I hope to suggest that what happened in St. Louis in the middle of the nineteenth century had a very direct and deep impact on what came to be known as America's most important indigenous philosophical movement. The Hegelian point to be kept in mind is that pragmatism, like any intellectual movement, did not appear on the scene from nowhere. It had—and has—a career and a history that must be taken into account as part of its meaning—as part of its being. In the midst of this career we find the voices of the St. Louis Movement leaving a permanent trace in the philosophical conversation we have come to call "pragmatism."

Notes

1. William James, *The Will to Believe* (New York: Dover Publications, 1956), 275.

2. Ibid., 295.

3. William James, *A Pluralistic Universe* (Lincoln: University of Nebraska Press, 1996), 87.

4. See James Good, *A Search for Unity in Diversity* (Lanham, Md.: Lexington Books, 2006).

5. Charles Peirce, *The Charles S. Peirce Papers*, The Houghton Library (Cambridge: Harvard University Microreproduction service, 1963-66). Cited by manuscript number MS L183.

6. Ibid.

7. Ibid.

8. William Torrey Harris, "Response," *JSP* 2, no. 2, (1868): 153-54.

9. Charles Peirce, *Collected Papers of Charles S. Peirce*, ed. Hartshorne and Weiss, vols. 1-6, ed. Burks, vols. 7-8 (Cambridge: Harvard University Press, 1963), citations by volume and paragraph number as is custom: 1.19.

10. Peirce, MS L183.

11. Peirce, *Collected Papers*, 8.38.

12. Peirce, *Collected Papers*, 6.218.

13. Ibid.

14. Peirce, *Collected Papers*, 8.272.

15. Peirce, *Collected Papers*, 5.436.

16. William James, *The Correspondence of William James*, vol. 5, ed. J. McDermott (Charlottesville: University of Virginia Press, 1997), 204.

17. Ralph Barton Perry, *The Thought and Character of William James*, vol. 2 (Boston: Little, Brown, and Company, 1935), 726.

18. Ibid., 770.

19. Thomas Davidson, *Education of the Wage-Earners* (Boston: Ginn, 1904), 37.

20. Perry, *The Thought and Character of William James*, 2:736.

21. Ibid., 2:739.

22. James, *A Pluralistic Universe,* 348.

23. Ibid., 359-60.

William T. Harris on "The Speculative"

Jerome P. Schiller, Washington University

On the 19th of January 1866, seven people, including Henry C. Brokmeyer, William T. Harris, and Denton J. Snider, met at the downtown office of Britton A. Hill in St. Louis "for the purpose of organizing a society for the promotion of Speculative Philosophy and its application."[1] Approximately one year later, at another meeting of the Society, the question was raised concerning the possible publication of a "journal of speculative philosophy" under the Society's auspices. The group assembled turned the publication decision over to a committee of five.[2] By the May 3, 1867, meeting of the Society, the newly appointed editor of the *Journal of Speculative Philosophy* had copies to distribute to members present.[3] From that date until the *JSP* ceased publication in December 1893, William T. Harris was the sole editor and a frequent contributor to the *Journal*.[4] A noteworthy feature turns up in both the founding document of the Society and in the title chosen for its *Journal* by its new members: the word *Speculative*. Of course, the word was in common use in English in the mid-nineteenth century, but, perhaps wisely, the editor did not leave it to his readers to determine its meaning for themselves. Rather, as the very first article in the first issue of the first volume of the *Journal*, he included a dense, five-page piece called "The Speculative."[5] His essay "Introduction to Philosophy," published in six parts in the first four issues of the first volume of the *Journal*, and the first and third issues of the second volume, provides a context for determining the meanings Harris had in mind in choosing a central role for the "Speculative" in philosophy.[6]

In section I, I focus on "The Speculative" and uncover the central characterization of the world that Harris holds to be true, a distinction of three levels of consciousness (the sensory, imaginative, and rational) and the three states of reality to which they correspond: a fragmented world of sense, the unified world of science, and—most real—the realm of self-determination. This three-level realm is, for Harris, the primary meaning of the Speculative. In section II, I consider the first and second levels of consciousness and their corresponding realities, both in general terms and with respect to scientific and philosophical theories of the day, which are grounded in the second level, specifically the theory of the correlation of forces, the problem of evolution, and the issue of freedom and determinism. In looking at these theories, I rely heavily on material from "Introduction," but I also turn to "Philosophy in Outline," which Harris wrote and published in the *Journal* in 1883, seventeen years after the appearance of "Introduction."[7] In some respects this essay is very close to the earlier one; in others it is markedly different. In section III, I consider the heart of Harris's metaphysics as developed in his notions of self-determination and negation, the highest level of the Speculative. I cite four very different descriptions of this complex state in an attempt to capture its multiple nuances—one from "The Speculative," one from "Introduction," and two from "Outline." In section IV, I consider several tools that Harris introduces to describe the multiple relations he finds between the different levels of his reality. These include such notions as mediation, distinction, comprehension, and, most importantly, the universal. In each of these logico-grammatical areas Harris moves in novel ways—often very differently in the two essays—but always interestingly, if not always convincingly. Finally, in section V, I summarize the earlier sections and conclude with a few critical comments on Harris's overall project.

I

HARRIS OPENS HIS DISCUSSION IN "THE SPECULATIVE" BY CITING FOUR well-known passages from classical philosophers: from Plato's *Republic*, Book VI, where Plato contrasts the speculative way of knowing in which the soul proceeds to an unhypothetical principle with the method of understanding; from Aristotle's *Metaphysics* XI, 7, where the philosopher shows that the self-moved is the first principle and identifies this with the Speculative and the being of God; from Aristotle's *De Anima* III, 5-8, where the philosopher shows the "active intellect" to be the highest form of knowing, as that which has itself as its own object and thus is infinite, and identical with the speculative result, the Absolute; and finally, from Spinoza's *Ethics* (Prop. xl. Schol. ii, and Prop. xliv., Cor.ii of pt. II) where the philosopher describes the Speculative as *scientia intuitiva*, the thinking of things under the form of eternity.[8]

Students of philosophy will be familiar with these passages, and they will immediately take Harris to be holding the Speculative, with which they are associated, in the highest esteem. But it is difficult to find a common core of meaning expressed by the passages, so his statements of praise lack focus. Harris proceeds to make a number of further statements about the Speculative, but they do not succeed any better than the four passages from classical philosophers in showing the reader precisely what it is. Thus he claims that there is near complete unanimity concerning the "transcendency" of the Speculative, that religion stands between art and philosophy as a mediator between the two, a sort of purgatory between the Inferno of sense and the Paradise of reason, but religion is forced to use ambiguous symbols to convey its insights. The most difficult problem, he claims, is to find a method adequate for the expression of the Speculative, the "Open Secret of the Universe."[9] For this method Harris turns again to Plato and his advice to start with immediate, but inadequate, principles and to remove these by ascending to the more adequate, until one reaches the first principles, absolutely universal and determined, the true infinite. Plato's approach, which Harris finds epitomized in the irony of Socrates, is, he claims, extremely difficult for a naïve mind to accept. "The soul of this method lies in the comprehension of the negative."[10] To develop his point Harris returns to the three kinds of knowing discussed by Plato and Spinoza.

The first stage of consciousness is that of sensuous knowing, in which objects are grasped as isolated from one another. The second stage is that in which objects are understood in their relations to one another. The third stage, which Harris characterizes as *self-determination*, is the highest, and the one which Harris calls "the speculative standpoint in its completeness."[11] I shall return to these characterizations—both to provide the fuller descriptions of them that Harris offers in "The Speculative" and to trace their roles in "Introduction" and "Outline" in sections II and III below.

Although Harris himself admits that his comments on the Speculative are "written in a rather desultory manner,"[12] they do provide the necessary framework for examining his use of the Speculative in his introductory essays.

II

Harris writes: "The first state of consciousness—that of immediate or sensuous knowing—seizes objects by themselves—isolatedly—without their relations; each seems to have validity in and for itself, and to be wholly positive and real. The negative is the mere absence of the real thing; and it utterly ignores it in its scientific activity."[13] But the second stage traces relations, and finds that things do not exist in immediate independence, but that each is related to others, and it comes to say that "Were a grain of sand to be destroyed, the universe would collapse."[14] It is a necessary consequent to the previous stage, for the reason that as soon as the first stage gets over its childish engrossment with the novelty of variety and attempts to seize the individual thing, it finds its characteristic marks or properties. But these consist invariably of relations to other things, and it learns that these properties, without which the thing could have no distinct existence, are the very destruction of its independence, since they are its complications with other things:

> In this stage the negative has entered and has full sway. For all that was before firm and fixed, is now seen to be, not through itself, but through others, and hence the being of everything is its negation. For if this stone exists only through its relations to the sun, which is *not* the stone but something else, then the being of this stone is its own negation. But the second stage only reduces all to dependence and finitude, and does not show us how any real, true, or independent being can be found to exist. It holds fast to the stage of mediation alone, just as the first stage held by the *immediate*. But the dialectic of this position forces it over into the third.[15]

Our ordinary macroscopic world, with its sticks and stones, is the focus of Harris's first and second states of consciousness. The first state, which he refers to as "sensuous" in the quotation from "The Speculative" above, isolates entities from one another, and this isolation ensures that they are not well understood. This is because everything in this world exists in an *environment.* Stones are heated by the sun, for example. They *are not* the sun, of course, but without taking the sun's heating into account, our understanding of the world would be inadequate. Harris calls the second state of consciousness, directed toward this more complex world, in which a stone must be related to the sun, "imaginative" and stresses the role of relationship here. This is the realm of natural science. Two important features characterize this level of consciousness and the world it uncovers. First, true scientific understanding increases with the scope of the material unified, and Harris does not seem to place any limits upon this. Second, the relationships characterizing the world are *negative* at core. Each of the things that contributes to a stone's being warmed—the sun and the air, for example—is part of the explanatory whole of which the stone is an element. They are not the stone, and yet each plays a central role in the being of the stone. Harris frequently uses the concept of "negative unity" to characterize entities on this second level. He introduces it with this example: an acid and a base each contains a lack of the other. When joined together and a salt is produced, Harris designates the salt a "negative unity" in that it negates the independence of the elements within it; likewise, in air, the independence of oxygen and nitrogen is ended.[16] In other contexts, he extends the use of the term to stress its unifying function and to broaden its applicability beyond the second level of consciousness. Thus, in later chapters of "Introduction," Harris frequently uses the term *negative unity* to refer to the totality that is created in the organic unification of diverse elements.

Harris does not hesitate to move beyond the consciousness and world of science to solve what appear to be scientific problems. In discussing some popular natural theories of his day, he returns repeatedly to consider the work of the correlationists.[17] He is anxious to show that those who feel that force exists only in radically individual natures are not the nominalists they believe themselves to be. This is because the only way such correlationists can talk about force is to talk about a generic persistent force. Obviously such talk leads them to the acceptance of a universal and is far away from the nominalism and materialism to which they profess. (In "Outline" Harris's move is even quicker. He simply defines the "persistent force" as the ground of individual forces "which supplies their energy and their changes."[18] This raises it to a higher level of reality, one above that of natural science.)

Harris takes up the theory of evolution in the course of his discussion of creation in the last two chapters of "Outline." "Science in our time interprets the phases of nature in the light of the principle of evolution. In the 'struggle for existence' one order develops into another."[19] Here Harris's step from his second level of consciousness, and its correlated scientific world, to the higher rational world is direct. The whole series of created things, stretching from inanimate objects through plants and animals to man, is necessarily determined by the second person of the trinity, as a consequence of its eternal derivation of being from the first and the annulment of that derivation.[20] Just as necessarily, immortality is bestowed on any animal that progresses beyond the capacities for recollection and fancy to that of generalization. The thrust of Harris's evolutionary theory is top-down: "Evolution prevails in nature, but it is not evolution of the lower to the higher through the unaided might of the lower. The lower order of being exists only in the process of evolution into the higher."[21]

As in the discussions of correlationism and the theory of evolution, Harris shows the same willingness to move beyond the ordinary world in his two very different treatments of the philosophical problem of freedom and determinism in "Introduction" and "Outline."

Determinism and Freedom in "Introduction"

Coherence of the entities and events that make up the scientific world is quite obviously a desideratum of natural science, but is this compatible with freedom? In a short chapter in "Introduction to Philosophy" titled "On Necessity, Chance, and Freedom," Harris attempts to find a place for freedom.[22] He offers a provocative argument against the deterministic position. First, he introduces change as a factor in his described world. He defines it as the passage of a potentiality into a reality (or, conversely, the passage of a reality into a potentiality). If, after the change, the same set of conditions necessitates both the old and the new states, then it cannot be said to necessitate one rather than the other, and chance or contingency must have participated in the state of the thing. However, when the thing changes, the totality also changes, and we are forced to admit that two *different* totalities are the conditions of the two different states. But what about the totality itself? There is nothing outside it to necessitate it, so it must necessitate *itself*. Necessity and the necessitated have thus turned out to be the same. But this, then, is not necessity, but rather spontaneity, which begins and ends with itself. As *necessitating*, it contains the potentiality on which it acts; as *necessitated*, it is the potentiality *plus* the limit its activity has fixed. "But we have here self-determination, and thus the *existence* of the universal in and for itself, which is the *ego*."[23] Details of his move remain obscure, but the thrust of his solution to the problem of determinism is, I think, clear. An adequately close examination of our world forces our attention to move to the higher realm of self-determination, the universal, and the ego.

Harris does not say explicitly how the moves of his argument provide a solution to the classical problem, though he does conclude with this observation: "The doctrine of necessity presupposes self-determination or freedom as the form of the total, and necessity is only one side . . . the *determined* side . . . of the process isolated. . . . Against this side stands the potentiality which . . . is called chance or contingency."[24]

Determinism and Freedom in "Philosophy in Outline"

In "Outline" Harris rethinks his discussion of freedom in "Introduction."[25] Although he assumes the same framework that underlies the discussion in the earlier article, he uses it in a radically different way. In this later version he carefully carves a path for the knower to ascend to a higher level of knowledge. He cites the extreme difficulty of following mathematical proofs if one is unfamiliar with the ordinary conceptions and combinations of mathematics. The truth of freedom cannot be seen from the second stage of knowledge, where environment and fate hold sway, just as fate cannot be seen from the first stage. In that stage one is conscious only of the object, in the second stage only of the environment, and it is not until one reaches the third stage that one is aware of logical presupposition. The way, Harris assures us, for passing from a lower to a higher stage is not difficult. Totality and self-determination await the knowledge only of one who has reached the highest stage. But, arrived there, it is obvious that determinism does not offer a true picture of things. Rather, freedom does. What holds under determinism is merely a flow of phenomena, not true self-activity.

Thus, the ultimate step that undercuts a deterministic model is there, at the end of both discussions. In the proof in "Introduction," freedom, self-determinism, and the ego, all familiar denizens of Harris's third realm, are things that follow from rational considerations underlying the logical properties of totality, necessity, and rationality-potentiality in the second realm. But freedom, totality, and self-determination come onto the scene in the discussion in "Outline" only when the individual is "converted" so that he is able to "see" them.

III

In both his solutions to the problem of determinism and freedom, Harris has appealed to a realm "above" that of ordinary scientific objects, a realm occupied by ego, mind, God, and freedom. This is not a realm completely separated from the first two realms. Indeed, as Harris prefers to put their relationship in "Outline," that higher realm is the logical ground, as well as ultimate explanation *(causa sui)* of the lower realms we encounter in space and time. In both "Introduction" and "Outline" Harris provides us with detailed accounts of the centerpiece of his philosophical system. He stresses its importance especially clearly in "Outline": "The insight into *Causa Sui* [self-activity] provides the most essential insight to obtain in all philosophy. . . . [I]t is the principle of life, of thought, of mind—the idea of a creative activity, and hence also the basis of theology as well as of philosophy."[26] Harris frequently refers to self-activity in the course of "The Speculative," "Introduction," and "Outline," and provides four separate descriptions of it. The first (in "The Speculative") is placed in no context other than its representing the third stage of consciousness; and the last ("Outline," ch. VII) is also placed in no special context. Both the second and third descriptions (in, respectively, "Introduction," ch. III, and "Outline," ch. IV) are introduced in a Kantian context. Following Kant's *Transcendental Aesthetic* and using Kant's well-known distinctions of the analytic-synthetic and the *a priori-a posteriori*, Harris establishes some central facts about the world, namely that space and time apply truly to the world in which we live—i.e., statements about them are synthetic—yet their truth is not traceable to experience (they are *a priori* in not being based upon experience.) Then, moving beyond Kant, Harris proposes that the basis of the power of space and time is in mind, or, as he prefers to put it in "Outline," *causa sui*. Thus he uncovers the highest realm, corresponding to his third level of consciousness.

> If things exist only in their relations, and relations are the negatives of things, then all that appears positive—all being—must rest upon negation. How is this? The negative is essentially a relative, but since it is the only substrate (for all is relative), it can relate only to itself. But self-relation is always identity, and here we have the solution of the previous difficulty. All positive forms, all forms of immediateness or being, all forms of identity, are self-relations, consisting of a negative or relative, relating to itself. But the most wonderful side of this is the fact that since this relation is that of the *negative,* it *negates* itself in its very relation, and hence its *identity* is a producing of *non*-identity. Identity and distinction are produced by the self-same process, and this *self-determination* is the origin of all identity and distinction likewise. **This is the speculative standpoint in its completeness.** It not only possesses speculative content, but is able to evolve a speculative system likewise. It is not only conscious of the principles, but of their method, and thus all is transparent.[27]

This is Harris's extended description of the highest, or third, realm of consciousness, from his essay "The Speculative." In some essentials, it echoes themes closely associated with the thought of the German philosopher, Hegel. This is not surprising, as Harris himself has credited Hegel with the *aperçu* "that the independent being, i.e., every really existing, separate entity, is self-determined."[28] Harris goes on to note that this *aperçu* "is the central point of speculative philosophy."[29] But it would be wrong, on this basis, to call the view expressed merely derivative.

Harris sets up here a dynamic interplay between the nature and status of an entity and the logical relationships between the concepts of relation-negation and identity-distinction that produces an unexpected economy, the self-same process producing opposite states. At the least this is a promising possibility in the field of metaphysics. This does not mean, however, that self-determination is unproblematic. A review of other formulations of the position may tell us why. Let us look at these, one from "Introduction" and two from "Outline."

Mind is transcendent, i.e. "something which time and space inhere in, rather than a somewhat conditioned by them."[30] What, then, constitutes its *a priori* activity? Harris argues that it is the *a priori* category of ego in its capacity of pure being that should focus our attention. In its first self-externalization (its first becoming object to itself) the ego must recognize itself. "This involves self-separation and then the annulling of this separation in the same act. For in knowing myself as an object I separate the ego from itself, but in the very act of *knowing* I make it identical again. Here are two negative processes involved in knowing, and these are indivisibly one:—first, the negative act of separation—secondly the negative act of annulling the separation by the act of recognition."[31]

In the first passage from "Outline," Harris moves economically from his identification of *causa sui* as the highest entity in the universe to its activity.[32] For a cause to influence an effect, it must separate its influence from itself. That is, it must self-separate. This form of self-activity is an infinite form of cause in that it is its own environment. Further, it is independent and consequently self-determined.

The context of the second passage is explicitly religious. The triune nature of God, i.e., the Christian Trinity, is the subject of this chapter. Harris undertakes to establish the relationships of the three Gods, holding that they form the "basis of the true theory of the existence of the world, and of man's freedom and immortality."[33] He begins at a now-familiar place: self-activity: "[S]elf-activity, or self-knowledge, or pure, absolute self-consciousness demands that the self-active should determine itself as self-active."[34] To be self-active and self-knowing the self-acting must be creative and create another which is the same as itself. The first absolute self-activity thus begets a second independent, free, perfect self-activity. The second, too, is creative. In knowing itself it creates a third equal in all respects to itself. Harris is here laying out the relationships that constitute the Christian Trinity. The first self-activity (God, the Father) creates a second perfect activity (God, the Son), who, together with the first, creates a third perfect activity, God, the Holy Spirit. The second God, because he is begotten, is passive, but because he has been made self-active from eternity, his passivity has been eternally annulled. It remains, nonetheless, an element in his self-knowledge. For this reason and thinking of his relation to the first God, the second God creates a world of finite beings extending from the most passive up to the most active. Of these beings, man alone is immortal and free. In this way the second God knows himself as a consummation and summit of creation, a procession. The third person of the Trinity proceeds from both the second and first persons and presides over the invisible church, the archetype of all institutions, which consists of innumerable souls connected by the bond of love.

Comparing these three passages with that from "The Speculative," each built around the concept of self-activity, we find striking similarities, but also one glaring difference. Negation, a crucial theme in the "Speculative" passage, is captured in the "Introduction" passage, in the "two negative processes" of separation and annulment, in the self-separation of the earlier passage from "Outline," and in the eternal annulling of the passivity of the Son (second God) in the Trinity account. Just as striking is the element that separates these accounts. In "The Speculative" passage reference to the actions of *persons* is limited to the use of "self" in the development of the argument. The overall impersonal tone of the argument, however, e.g., the references to "entities" and "things," shows that this use of self carries no *personal* implications. This tone is very different from that of the other passages. The "Introduction" passage intimately involves ego in the story, and furthermore brings the "I" in as well (e.g., in knowing myself as an object). Furthermore, the concept of annulment would appear to involve the interactions of persons. The first passage from "Outline" also seems to call upon the action or outlook of a person in the distinction of a cause and its influence. Even if such a separation may be viewed logically, I think that it is close to vacuous in a nonpersonal context. And finally, with respect to the use of self-determination to lay out the relationships of the Gods in the Trinity, there may be too many persons in this account for it to be at all explanatory.

What is to be done about this conflict? Clearly, Harris subscribes to all four versions. There is abundant evidence in both "Introduction" and "Outline" that Harris consistently held a strong conviction that independent entities, particularly the highest, are persons. And, of course, using his position concerning self-activity to ground his account of the Trinity strongly suggests the personal interpretation. It is disappointing to see his thought move in this way toward the personal, for the impersonal approach of "Speculative" is more promising.

This completes my discussion of the three levels of consciousness that constitute Harris's explication of the Speculative in his early essay of that name. But there are several topics to which Harris devotes careful attention that serve to fill in features of the universe he has constructed. I turn now to discuss these in section IV.

IV

In this section I shall look at mediation, comprehension, distinction, and the universal, all logico-grammatical tools Harris uses to relate the different realms of being that he has distinguished. His discussions also introduce material that fills in gaps in my presentation of his universe thus far.

In chapter six of "Introduction," Harris sets up a contradiction between the mediate and the immediate in the lower two realms. According to him, undue reliance on the mediate leads to over-reliance on abstraction. Abstraction is necessary for knowledge, both theoretical and practical—given the constitution of the world—but it must be tempered. Immediate knowledge is impossible in itself, and as phenomenal, it yields a mere abstraction from the concrete whole. The solution lies in self-determination. This is a system or process that is both mediate and immediate: mediate because it is a process, immediate because it is its own mediation.

In chapter seven Harris uses the tool of negative unity to define "comprehension," the complete thought that includes both the elements ("moments," as he calls them, after Hegel) of an entity and their negative unity, which holds them together as a self-determined totality. Harris uses the concept of an idea, by which Hegel means a comprehension (system) of comprehensions, to discuss a variety of universes suggested by both philosophers and by Christian thinkers. Throughout, his touchstone is "the highest point of view in philosophy—true multiplicity and true unity coexisting."[35]

Harris considers three types of distinction: difference, opposition, and contradiction in chapter nine. The general thrust of his formal discussion of the third, or speculative, theory of distinction is that self-determination (contradiction) is the ultimate principle of thought (and being), that *distinction* arises in the act of self-identification, and *identity* in the act of self-distinction. Both are involved in the same process, which he here calls the concept of the *universal*.[36] The thrust of his argument in the sub-chapter "Scientific Deduction of the Forms of Distinction" is that at core difference is based on opposition and opposition is based on contradiction, understood here as self-negativity. Harris says:

> Contradiction, or self-negativity, has the following obvious characteristics:
> (a) The relation of the negative to itself is one of identity;
> (b) But since it is a negative, it produces distinction by the same relation.
> (c) Hence, in its contradiction it preserves itself, and is its own ground.[37]

He turns, at this point, to the "Laws of Thought," and points out their defects, whether applied to objects or processes. Central here is their inapplicability to the world with its real concreteness and relativity. The principles of Identity, Contradiction, and the Excluded Middle falsely abstract from the world. "Speculative insight *always* regards the process,—sees all things in their *genesis*, and thus can comprehend synthesis as well as analysis."[38]

It is surprising that, sixteen years later, in chapter eight of "Outline," Harris had no difficulty in commending these laws and even found them to illumine his own universe. He finds the principle of Identity, A is A, to express the category of being, hence the first stage of consciousness. The principle of Contradiction, not-A is not identical with A, has an explicit reference to the environment and to the mutual exclusion and finitude of both A and not-A. Contradiction thus falls clearly in the second stage of consciousness. The principle of Excluded Middle, A either is or is not, or in the case of two mutual contradictories, we can affirm the existence of only one. This adds the concept of totality to identity and contradiction, and thus relates to the ground or logical condition, the third stage of consciousness. To these traditional laws of thought Harris adds the principle of sufficient reason. He claims that "through it we perceive the necessity of *causa sui,* or self-activity as the sufficient reason for any causal action whatever."[39] Thus every level of his universe, including the highest, is reflected in the laws he dismissed as relatively worthless sixteen years previously.

This excursus into some logico-grammatical features of Harris's works yields several important results. In general we observe Harris's unswerving focus on his central metaphysical insight: all roads lead, as it were, through mediation, comprehension, or distinction to self-determination. More particularly, we find first, in the "Scientific Deduction" of chapter IX, a brief back-up proof that mirrors that in "The Speculative" and exhibits succinctly the roles that negativity, identity, and distinctness play in establishing the highest reality.[40] Second, we see an enrichment of this highest reality as it becomes melded to wholeness and totality through Harris's extension of the concept of negative unity to the third level of consciousness. Third, and this particularly in Harris's rejection of the use of the Laws of Thought in "Introduction," is his stress on truly rational thought focusing on process over product in gaining an adequate insight into reality. These features are, to a degree, foreshadowed in the description of the second level of consciousness. The world of science is a totality, highly integrated, the inhabitants of which are concrete, as are their practices. And of course the emphasis on the negative and relation adumbrate, though hardly yield, the central insight of the highest realm.

Undoubtedly, in Harris's eyes, the most important of those entities that bridge the gaps among the realms of reality are universals. The great value this tool has in Harris's estimation is evident in the fact that he defers its formal treatment until the last chapter of "Introduction," and that he closes that chapter with a summary of all the preceding chapters, in which he undertakes to show that "each *aperçu* [chapter] was a phase of the universal, and luminous for that very reason."[41]

Harris concludes this culminating chapter of "Introduction," "The universal is to be reached as the form of speculative insight. . . . [It is] . . . the key to all thinking and being."[42] But what does he mean by universal? He does not mean what is obtained by abstracting common features from objects and actions of ordinary experience. Such abstractions are accidental, possibly subjective, and the words that are associated with them and their related concepts are, according to him, figments of the mind. No, we must rather approach the world dynamically, and not statically. We must see that particulars in the world have defects and potentialities that can be realized only by transcending this realm. They need to be related to the beyond. The existence of each entity is thus *self-transcending*.[43] To illustrate this point Harris cites the examples of (1) heaviness as part of each particular object's nature, (2) heavenly bodies that constitute a system which is larger than any component of the system, and (3) every individual in space and time that is what it is through its relations. In each case the entity is an embodied contradiction. Thus, a body is not heavy, but at the same time it is heavy; the earth is not the sun, but at the same time it is the sun; every individual is not related, but it is related. For Harris, then, contradiction here requires transcendence, since this is a way of escaping contradiction. So, in short, what is, is the universal.[44] Each particular is, then, a universal. Harris also calls it a *phenomenon*. There are two sides to the nature of a phenomenon, or universal. First, there is the deficiency, that is the activity of the including totality (the "negative unity"). Second, the entity is itself negative to its including totality, for it can lose its independence if the totality has full sway. Harris adds that the entity would not be phenomenal, i.e., transient, unless the negative unity of the including total annulled the real and caused the potential to become real. He further claims that here also arises the manifestation of the including totality, what Harris calls the "generic." And thus arises the "only true individual, for it alone abides and does not pass over into another, as the particular of space and time does continually."[45]

The similarities between this account of the universal and the accounts of self-determination at other points in Harris's essays are not accidental. Self-contemplation is often said to rest upon a double negativity. In the account of universals there is also a double negativity: the negative unity of the including totality and the negativity required to sustain the particular against the force of that totality. Second, in central descriptions of self-determination there is the *annulment* characteristic of the separation. Here, the annulment of the real and replacement by the potential serves to stabilize the process.

To the extent that this parallel really holds, it provides strong internal support for Harris's system. Universals are easily attached to the ego, since their mode of being has been shown to be virtually the same. Harris has established a version of a universal that is highly effective in the universe.

V

In "The Speculative" Harris bases his characterization of the Speculative on his theory of consciousness. He divides consciousness into three levels: sensuous, imaginative, and rational, each attached to a different level of reality: isolated objects, the world of natural science, and freedom, God, and the ego. These realms gain their natures from their relationship to the primary inhabitant of the highest realm, self-determination. Thus God and the ego are instances of self-determination, while isolated objects and scientific objects are *dependent* upon *independent* entities with self-determination. The centrality of self-determination does not stop here, however. Logical tools such as mediation, comprehension (totality), the laws of thought, and universals gain their force from relationship to this central idea. Harris's early description of self-determination captures this fruitfulness: "This is the speculative standpoint in its completeness. It . . . possesses speculative content, but is able to evolve a speculative system likewise."[46] Harris may have learned about the importance of self-determination from others, in particular from Henry Brokmeyer, but the complex system with which he has buttressed it, and on which a good part of his reputation lies, is surely his own.

Notes

1. Kurt F. Leidecker, ed., *Record Book of the St. Louis Philosophical Society, Founded 1866* (Lewiston, N.Y.: Edwin Mellen Press, 1990), 45.

2. Kurt F. Leidecker, *Yankee Teacher* (New York: Philosophical Library, 1946), 324-25.

3. Leidecker, *Record Book*, 87. There is a well-established story concerning the origin of the *JSP*, possibly apocryphal, but nonetheless worth repeating. William T. Harris, it seems, had submitted an article titled "The Speculative" to the *North American Review.* When it was rejected and returned, he read it to some colleagues at the St. Louis Philosophical Society, along with the negative (and colorful) editorial comments that accompanied it. On concluding the reading, he is said to have exclaimed: "We will start our own journal, then." Quoted by Dorothy Rogers in *Transactions of the C. S. Peirce Society* 40 (2004), 547. According to D. J. Snider, he said, bringing down his closed fist, "Now I'm going to start a Journal myself." Quoted in Edward L. Schaub, "Harris and the *Journal of Speculative Philosophy*," in Edward L. Schaub, ed., *William Torrey Harris, 1835-1935* (Chicago: Open Court Publishing Co., 1936), 54.

4. Schaub, ed., *William Torrey Harris*, 51.

5. Harris, "The Speculative," *JSP* 1 (1867): 2-6.

6. William T. Harris, "Introduction to Philosophy," hereafter "Introduction," in *JSP* 1 (1867): 57-60, ch. I, 116-21, chs. II-IV, 187-90, chs. V-VI, 236-40, chs. VII-VIII; *JSP*2 (1868): 51-55, ch. IX, 176-81, ch. X.

7. Harris, "Philosophy in Outline," hereafter "Outline," in *JSP* 17 (1883): 296-316, chs. I-VII, 337-56, chs. VIII-XI.

8. Harris, "The Speculative," *JSP*1, 2a-b.

9. Ibid., 2b-3b.

10. Ibid., 4a.

11. Ibid., 5a.

12. Ibid., 5a.

13. Ibid., 4a.

14. Ibid., 4b.

15. Ibid., 4a-b.

16. "Introduction," *JSP*1, 121b.

17. Ibid., 120b.

18. "Outline," 338.

19. Ibid., 347.

20. Ibid., 353.

21. Ibid., 350.

22. "Introduction," *JSP*1, 187-90.

23. Ibid., 188b. Harris uses arguments very similar to this at other points in his essays: in chapter four of "Introduction" to establish the self-recognition of the self-determined entity, and in "The Speculative" to show self-determination to be the origin of all identity and difference. In each of these discussions Harris uncovers an unexpected identity of apparently contrasting concepts. In this passage concerning freedom it is necessity and the necessitated; in the passage in chapter four of "Introduction" it is the determining and the determined; in the passage from "The Speculative" it is, with a slight twist, identity and distinction. What he does with this set-up varies in each case, but it is always, as in the example here, challenging. (See below, p. 47-48, for a quotation of the argument from "The Speculative," plus commentary.)

24. "Introduction," *JSP*1, 188b.

25. See "Outline," 312-16.

26. "Outline," 304.

27. Harris, "The Speculative," *JSP*1, 4b-5a; my emphasis.

28. "Introduction," *JSP*1, 121a.

29. Ibid.

30. "Introduction," *JSP*1, 117.

31. Ibid., 113.

32. "Outline," 303-4.

33. Ibid., 319.

34. Ibid.

35. "Introduction," *JSP*1, 238.

36. "Introduction," *JSP*2, 51.

37. Ibid., 53.

38. Ibid., 55.

39. "Outline," 340.

40. "Introduction," *JSP*2, 52.

41. Ibid., 179b.

42. Ibid., 179a.

43. Ibid., 176.

44. My understanding has been that Harris has already effected the combination of the separate items that exist on the first level of consciousness by showing how they are related to one another in his description of the genesis of the second level—by their attraction into larger wholes, those wholes possibly growing as extensive as the entire (determined) universe. In that explanation there is no mention of the beyond. I see no obvious difference between "defects" in that second stage description and here.

45. "Introduction," *JSP*2, 177.

46. Harris, "The Speculative," *JSP*1, 5a.

Mentor as Blessing/Curse

Marietta Kies and the Problem of Derivative Identity

Dorothy Rogers, Montclair State University

It is almost impossible to adequately discuss the legacy of William Torrey Harris and the St. Louis Movement without recognizing his immense support of the educational and career advancement of women—which he gave in myriad ways, as superintendent of schools in St. Louis, leader of philosophy and literature clubs in that city, editor of the *Journal of Speculative Philosophy*, and founder of the Concord Summer School of Philosophy and Literature. In fact, it is tempting to spend the bulk of this paper providing an overview of all the women whose careers Harris helped advance through his support and encouragement, both personally and professionally. But it will have to suffice first to give you just a glimpse of some of the more significant of Harris's female colleagues. I will then focus on one woman in particular, Marietta Kies (pronounced like "pies," not like "keys"), who was helped immeasurably by Harris, but at the same time was somewhat burdened by her status as his disciple.

Harris is still fairly well known as a leader in American education. And it is largely because the movement he led in St. Louis was so concerned with education that he and his contemporaries were especially important and empowering for women. Women's career options in the last third of the nineteenth century were extremely limited, after all. And as an egalitarian, Harris provided ample opportunity for intellectual women to flourish within his circle of educators and philosophical idealists. No fewer than twenty of the scores of women who knew Harris through his work as an educator and philosopher became well-known as feminist educators, as activists, or as philosophical thinkers.

Many of Harris's female colleagues in the St. Louis public school system were also members of his several philosophy and pedagogy clubs—women like Susan Blow, director of the first free, public, and ongoing successful kindergarten program in the U.S., and Anna Brackett, the first woman in the country to head a secondary school and a teacher-education theorist, as well as a feminist. Grace Bibb, Mary Beedy, Amelia Fruchte, Gertrude Garrigues, Ellen Mitchell, and Ella Morgan were each active in Harris's educational and philosophical circles in St. Louis, and achieved success as educators, writers, and/or philosophical thinkers.

Some of these women as well as others from other regions of the country contributed to Harris's *Journal of Speculative Philosophy* from the year it first appeared in print in 1867 until its last issue in 1888 (which, because of demands on Harris's time, including a new job as U.S. commissioner of education, did not appear in print until 1893). Susan Blow, Anna Brackett, and Ellen Mitchell contributed regularly to the *JSP*.

Women beyond St. Louis, like Julia Gulliver, Julia Ward Howe, and May Wright Sewall, each wrote just a handful of articles for the journal. But in each case, the woman herself had a heavy writing, teaching, and/or research agenda outside of her work for the *JSP*. Julia Gulliver was just the third woman to earn the Ph.D. in philosophy in the nineteenth century (Smith College, 1888) and would later become the president of Rockford College. Julia Ward Howe was a well-known and popular women's rights activist, a writer, and an invited speaker at the Concord School. Sewall was a teacher and, as a member of the Chicago Women's Club, advocated for the inclusion of both African American and Jewish women into that elite and powerful organization. She was also an associate of Jane Addams, and with Addams she developed an especially high commitment to peace activism.

Later on many of these women made the trip to the East Coast to study with Harris at the Concord Summer School of Philosophy and Literature in Massachusetts—Bibb, Beedy, Fruchte, and Mitchell among them. Numerous others became his students at Concord, one of the few places where women could study philosophy at roughly the graduate level at a time when most universities were still closed to them. Lucia Ames (later Mead) and Marietta Kies are among a number of women who met and studied with Harris at Concord, and both became prominent in their chosen lines of work: Ames in pacifist theory/activism and Kies in academic philosophy.

Harris developed a genuine disciple in Marietta Kies (1853-99). She was the seventh American woman to earn a doctoral degree in philosophy, and she became one of only a handful of women (to my knowledge, only three) to teach philosophy at a co-educational college or university before 1900 (Butler College in Indianapolis).

Kies's first publication, *Introduction to the Study of Philosophy* (1889), was a compilation of Harris's articles and lectures that she worked on while studying with him at the Concord School. She received a great deal of praise for this work, which reviewers said presented Harris's views to a wider audience in a way that was systematic and clear. Some said she did a better job of expressing Harris's views than he did himself! While this book was in press, Kies applied to the University of Michigan, with a letter of recommendation from Harris, to study philosophy under George Sylvester Morris and John Dewey, becoming the first woman at Michigan to earn a Ph.D. in the discipline.

In the 1890s, Kies began her work on political altruism. Her theory drew on the early American, Harris-style interpretations of Hegel regarding the nature and role of the home, school, church, and state, and in that sense is somewhat predictable. Yet it also incorporated aspects of the ideas of progressivism and socialism that are novel, and which Harris shied away from. Most intriguing for feminists today is the way in which Kies's thought anticipated the feminist ethic of care that would develop almost one hundred years later in the 1980s.

At the center of Kies's work was a distinction between the ethic of Justice or egoism, and the ethic of Grace, which she also sometimes referred to as Charity, or altruism. The first is prevalent in the public worlds of business and politics. It provides a thin layer of protection to all individuals based on a conception of rights. The second is most prevalent in the worlds of home and church. It provides a more full, holistic means of empowering individuals and groups to become agents in their own right. But if society is to run smoothly, if the state is to be truly rational, in Kies's Hegelian view, Justice and Grace must complement each other in all realms of human activity—in politics, business, church, home, and school.

Despite the originality of Kies's theory of altruism, it did not receive the attention it deserved in her lifetime, because it was considered derivative of Harris's ideas. Josiah Royce first made this claim in a brief notice of her first book, *The Ethical Principle.*[1] Caroline K. Sherman, who was advocating for women's participation at the 1893 World's Fair, also dismissed Kies as a viable speaker because her work was too similar to that of Harris. This is curious, because, aside from the compilation of Harris's articles and lectures that Kies published in 1889, her work strikes a note that is decidedly original and distinct from anything that Harris put into print, aside from a short article on altruism that he published in the *Christian Union.*[2] Granted, the basic outline of ideas in this article is similar to what we later see in Kies's *Ethical Principle* and *Institutional Ethics*, but these were each full-scale discussions of altruism, the second nearly three hundred pages in length.[3] At the risk of hyperbole, to write off Kies's theory of altruism as merely derivative of Harris is like declaring Plato's work derivative of Socrates. On the subject of altruism, Harris had written so little that there really is no basis for saying that Kies was merely miming her mentor in writing these books.

So how can this be? How could Kies's work have been labeled derivative of her mentor's when Harris wrote just one short article on altruism and no full-length books on political philosophy at all? At the root of this problem is the blessing/curse dynamic of a woman's mentor/discipleship relationship with a prominent man in the field. Without Harris, Kies may very literally have had no academic career at all. She was from a poor farm family in the northeast corner of Connecticut. For financial reasons, she struggled to finish school, and she was not able to complete her college degree until she was twenty-eight years old. Then, at the age of thirty-four, she entered the graduate program in philosophy at the University of Michigan, which had only recently been opened to women, with a letter from William Torrey Harris in hand. At the same time, even after establishing herself as a full-time professor (which Harris had never managed to do) and at a co-educational institution (which only one other woman had managed to do; Christine Ladd-Franklin taught at Johns Hopkins, but not full-time) and putting forth two original works on altruism, she was still seen as first and foremost Harris's student, not a thinker in her own right.

This is partly due to contingencies of birth and temperament. Kies was nearly twenty years younger than Harris, and early in their mentor/disciple relationship, when he was at his most influential, she was not able to distinguish herself from him. In addition, Harris was, by all accounts, almost irresistibly gregarious, as well as zealous about his philosophical interests. Any student could easily have been overshadowed by him. Kies was spoken of as a calm, steady, earnest individual who thought before she spoke and who always had the interests of others in mind. In personality, then, she was more like John Dewey than she was W. T. Harris, and without the benefit of a long lifespan on her side, she did not make a splash, as such, with her books and ideas, as Harris seemed to do spontaneously and which Dewey did in his deliberate and deliberative way over time.

Another factor, which every fan of the St. Louis Movement laments, is the fact that after Harris accepted the position of commissioner of education with the U.S. government, he lost influence in philosophical circles as they became increasingly academic. This is exactly the point at which Kies had begun to establish herself professionally, in the 1890s. So the previously close association she'd had with him was, if anything, a bit of a deficit for Kies. Add to this the fact that, unfortunately, she died just five years after publishing her second book on altruism, and we have a script for "how to ensure a thinker gets forgotten." The one person who could have championed her work was now too occupied with policy making and too distant from the academy to indulge in genuine philosophy. And even if he had been able to cheer Kies on in her work, it is unlikely many of her male colleagues in colleges and universities would have listened very carefully, given the fact that he and his ideas had fallen out of vogue by that time.

A couple of feminist factors come into play in the derivative identity problem as well. Kies was a woman who ventured out of the normal terrain that women in this era generally remained in within the discipline—educational theory, psychology, aesthetics, philosophy of religion, or women's rights discussions. So in some sense, neither her male nor her female colleagues knew what to make of her and her work.

Yet, the discerning critic, or internally critical feminist, will say, "Ah! But we have Mary Whiton Calkins and Christine Ladd-Franklin. They were appreciated as serious thinkers in their day and are at least somewhat remembered/recognized today." I will concede this is true. Their work was largely in the subfields of logic and metaphysics, which are often considered the more prestigious—even more valid—branches of the discipline. They also both did some work in the field of psychology, then a new branch of philosophy. Lucky them! They wrote on the right things at the right time, and they distanced themselves enough from their male counterparts to avoid being dismissed as mere "echoes" of their male teachers. Yet, we must keep in mind that the mood was such in academic circles at this time that Christine Ladd-Franklin had to fight at every turn not to be excluded from psychology meetings. Her male colleague, E. B. Titchener, who was a leading figure in psychology at the time, was so hostile to women in the field that in preparing for an upcoming conference he complained that Ladd-Franklin had insisted on being included. "Possibly she will [force] us to meet—like rabbits—in some dark place underground."[4] Ladd-Franklin was unapologetically feminist, because she had to be. And Calkins, who found herself denied her doctoral degree because of Harvard's policy against credentialing women, did not shy away from feminist thinking and writing either—again, because she found she had to do so.

Meanwhile, Kies developed ideas within political philosophy that were original and groundbreaking, particularly from a feminist standpoint. But she didn't make any feminist waves, as Ladd-Franklin did in her political dealings with male colleagues and as Mary Whiton Calkins occasionally did in her written work. In contrast to these two contemporaries, we see charges that Kies's work lacked originality, that her theory was too familiar, because her mentor talked a good deal about matters she systematically wrote about. Perhaps Kies's distance from feminism was actually part of the problem.

Obviously this leads us to a final feminist point: Kies was not strongly feminist, so she did not approach her work, or her role as a woman in the academy, as a women's rights matter. In a sense, Kies's work was actually too novel, too nuanced, and her colleagues were simply unprepared to accept and interpret it. Therefore, it was—plain and simple—

misunderstood. For instance, she went to great lengths to make it clear that in her system, Justice and Grace were to complement each other. Both principles were to be incorporated into public/political decision making so that they worked equally, in tandem. Even so, at least one of her contemporaries misunderstood her theory and rendered Grace a secondary principle, one that could be used to supplement Justice when needed. Similarly, another determined that her principle of Grace, as a religious ethic, had little place in the world of politics.[5] Clearly the intellectual world she was a part of was not ready to talk about blurring the lines between the public and private realms in the way that Kies was advocating. And she never made the next step that "ethic of care" theorists made eighty years after her death, the step that would connect her altruistic ideas to feminist ideals of help and nurture. Ironically, Harris, who was a strong supporter of women's rights, quite likely would have encouraged her in this regard. But because she failed (or perhaps refused) to see herself in a feminist context, the opportunity to establish her ideas as truly distinct and original (sans claims of derivation) was lost.

In short, if there have been factors that have contributed to William Torrey Harris's fading from cultural memory in recent decades, they have been compounded for Marietta Kies. Yet her work has serious merit, particularly with its feminist implications, so it should not—must not—be forgotten. And William Torrey Harris, who literally made the careers of Kies and women like her possible, is to be posthumously thanked and congratulated for inspiring her as he did. We simply need to retroactively take away the extra credit that he received for work that she did (albeit after being inspired and encouraged by him) which Harris simply did not deserve.

NOTES

1. Marietta Kies, *The Ethical Principle* (Ann Arbor: Inland Press, 1892).

2. In "The Church and the State in Relation to the School," *Christian Union* (Dec. 1, 1887), Harris briefly sketched out some of the ideas that Kies then developed fully in *The Ethical Principle.*

3. Marietta Kies, *Institutional Ethics* (Boston: Allyn & Bacon, 1894).

4. E. B. Titchener, quoted in Elizabeth Scarborough and Laurel Furumoto, *Untold Lives: The First Generation of American Psychologists* (New York: Columbia University Press, 1987), 126.

5. See W. B. Elkin, "Review of Kies, Institutional ethics," *Philosophical Review* 4, no. 4 (1895): 459-60, and Charles Cook, "Review of Kies, The ethical principle and its application in state relations," *Philosophical Review* 1, no. 6 (1892): 673-75.

Absolute Speculation

The St. Louis Hegelians and the Question of American National Identity

*Matt Erlin, Washington University**

INCLUDED AMONG THE PAPERS IN THE WILLIAM TORREY HARRIS ARCHIVE at the Missouri Historical Society is a manuscript from the 1850s entitled, "Do the signs of the times indicate a degeneration of American character?" In the essay Harris responds to his own question with a resounding "no" and offers a succession of examples to demonstrate America's continued intellectual and moral progress: two-thousand steamboats now ply waters previously navigated only by canoe, three-hundred daily newspapers have replaced the three that were available in the early republic, and perhaps most importantly, "throughout the land by every murmuring waterfall the ceaseless hum of the spindle or the ring of the mechanic's hammer is heard."[1] In response to those critics who detect a decline in religiosity and a corruption of morals, Harris contrasts early Puritan theocracy and superstition with the more recent spirit of Christian tolerance. Only the barbarous institution of slavery continues to mar America's great democratic experiment. According to Harris, however, it will soon suffer the fate of "its kindred institutions of the dark ages."[2]

William Torrey Harris was later to become the most famous of the three core members of the group now known as the St. Louis Hegelians. As legend has it, the group came into being one winter night in 1858,

* "Absolute Speculation: The St. Louis Hegelians and the Question of American National Identity" by Matt Erlin. First published in *German Culture in Nineteenth-Century America: Reception, Adaptation, Transformation*, ed. Lynne Tatlock and Matt Erlin (Rochester, N.Y.: Camden House, 2005), 89-106. Reprinted by permission.

after a meeting of the St. Louis Literary and Philosophical Society at the Mercantile Library. Harris, who had come to St. Louis in 1857 with the intention of teaching shorthand, was approached and befriended by Henry Conrad Brokmeyer, a rough-hewn Prussian emigrant and self-taught proponent of German idealism. Brokmeyer allegedly convinced Harris of Hegel's preeminence among modern philosophers, and shortly thereafter they and a few others began meeting to engage in a systematic study of his work.[3] At the urging and with the financial support of the others, Brokmeyer also undertook a translation of Hegel's *Wissenschaft der Logik* (referred to as the *Larger Logic*), a project that would occupy him periodically for the rest of his life. Though the translation was never published, the book itself played a key role in the self-definition of the group, and of Harris in particular.[4] The onset of the Civil War led to the dissolution of this initial company, but when Brokmeyer returned to St. Louis after the war, he and Harris founded the St. Louis Philosophical Society, which served as the organizational home of the movement until Harris left to participate in the Concord Summer School of Philosophy in 1880. In the mid-1860s they were also joined by Denton Snider, the third prominent member of an inner circle of committed Hegelians.[5]

While the American reception of Hegel neither began in nor was limited to St. Louis, Harris, Brokmeyer, and Snider were without a doubt the most influential popularizers and disseminators of Hegelian philosophy in nineteenth-century America.[6] Brokmeyer's impact was limited largely to those with whom he had personal contact. He served as the intellectual inspiration behind the entire movement, but he published only a few essays, and the manuscript of his monumental translation still gathers dust in the Missouri Historical Society archives. Snider and Harris, however, published hundreds of books and articles on philosophical, cultural, and political topics, many of which deal directly with Hegel or at least bear the stamp of his influence.[7] Both were also active public lecturers and educators; Snider had a close connection to the kindergarten movement and Harris, after serving as superintendent of the St. Louis schools and then teaching at the Concord Summer School, was appointed in 1889 to the position of United States Commissioner of Education. Probably the group's most significant contribution to the dissemination of Hegelian ideas, however, was the *Journal of Speculative*

Philosophy. Founded and edited by Harris and generally acknowledged to be the first truly philosophical periodical published in the United States, the journal appeared regularly from 1867 through 1887. It devoted considerable space to both the presentation and interpretation of Hegelian philosophy and of German idealism more generally. It also served as something of a springboard for a new generation of American philosophers, including Charles Sanders Peirce, William James, and John Dewey.

For those cultural and intellectual historians who have taken an interest in this group of amateur philosophers, the question as to why Hegel exerted such a pull in late-nineteenth-century St. Louis has been a frequent topic of discussion, and the answer has often focused on the Hegelian's desire to overcome the national divisions that had led to the Civil War and remained unresolved in its aftermath.[8] There can be no doubt that the war became for these thinkers the paradigmatic event for the application of Hegelian frameworks to American history, but the basic mindset that motivated their fascination with Hegel can in fact already be discerned in Harris's early essay on the American character. Its combination of optimism haunted by uncertainty goes a long way toward explaining all three thinkers' devotion to German idealism, and to Hegel more specifically. Hegel himself had remarked in his *Philosophy of History* that "America is . . . the land of the future," and the Hegelians took this claim to heart, even if they had a rather different interpretation of what it meant from Hegel himself.[9] His thought made it possible to hold on to a belief in American progress and in America's world-historical mission even in the face of contrary evidence, not only in the case of the Civil War and the chaos of reconstruction, but also the unsettling effects of late-nineteenth-century immigration, industrialization, and urbanization. It was the power of the historical dialectic that ultimately constituted the primary source of Hegel's appeal. The dialectic allowed the Hegelians to reframe even historical catastrophes as necessary stages in a progression toward an ultimate reconciliation, and it continued to inform the writings of the members of the society long after they went their separate ways.

The central role of the dialectic and of Hegel's concept of negation has not been overlooked by those who have written on the movement. As one early commentator noted in 1935, "Throughout the record there sounds the rumble of the Hegelian *triadic movement*."[10] In the introduction to *The American Hegelians*, an anthology of writings by both the St. Louis and Ohio Hegelians, William Goetzmann traces Hegel's attractiveness back to the fact that "virtually every event in nineteenth-century America could be fitted into the ongoing dialectic and the unfolding process of the concrete universal."[11] Others have discussed the role of the dialectic in the Hegelians' contribution to the shift from individualism to institutionalism in nineteenth-century American thought, as well as in their arguments about the unique role of St. Louis and the Middle West as a site of mediation between the values of the North and South.[12] Most recently, James Good has returned to these topics in a detailed investigation of the three main figures' responses to the Civil War, in which he elucidates their comparisons of Napoleon and Lincoln and their view of the conflict as an important moment in the unfolding of the World-Spirit.[13]

The following contribution takes up the topic of the dialectic in order to shed light on a particular aspect of its appropriation that has in fact been neglected and that may also help to illuminate the high stakes of cultural transfer in late-nineteenth-century America. Much of the commentary on Harris and company has tended to present their use of the dialectic as simplistic, as a mere reconciliation of opposites. The St. Louis Hegelians themselves no doubt contributed to such a reading, indulging on various occasions in a rather carefree application of the thesis-antithesis-synthesis model of development, a model that many Hegel scholars oppose in principle as a simplistic reduction of Hegel's thought. Snider, for example, in his 1920 history of the movement, presents the "Great Illusion" of St. Louis's rise to prominence as thesis, the founding of the Philosophical Society as antithesis, and the building of the Eads Bridge as a kind of synthesis. He also relates the rather more callous example of Brokmeyer describing the great Chicago fire as the negation of Chicago's original negation of St. Louis, an event that would allow St. Louis to re-establish its supremacy.[14] Despite such frivolities, however, Harris and Snider, at least in their early writings, demonstrate a rather sophisticated understanding of Hegel's historical dialectic, in particular of the crucial role played by self-consciousness in the unfolding of spirit, or *Geist.* Recognizing the importance of self-consciousness in these early texts, moreover, opens up a new perspective on the appeal of Hegel and the concerns of the Hegelians. Snider and Harris not only used Hegel to make sense of the chaotic situation in America following the war, but also to provide an explanation for what they saw as a crucial flaw in the American character, one that arguably gave rise to the chaos in the first place. As we shall see, both Harris and Snider are deeply concerned with what they view as America's intellectual immaturity, an immaturity that they believe has prevented citizens from grasping the true nature of the country's historical mission.

Snider and the Self-Conscious Republic

In 1874 Denton Snider published a pamphlet entitled *The American State*, which consisted of a series of articles that had appeared in the St. Louis periodical *The Western* in the preceding few years. At the time Snider was teaching high school philosophy and had just emerged from a six-year immersion in the works of Hegel. He would later shift away from philosophy to publish primarily on literary and cultural topics, from Goethe's *Faust* to the psychology of architecture.[15] Although Snider never abandoned Hegelian conceptual frameworks entirely, these early articles are unique in their faithfulness to the philosopher. They also document Snider's profound discouragement with the conditions of American political and social life in the wake of the Civil War, in particular with the extent of corruption among public officials. In his words, "there is today, without doubt, a far greater portion of the people of the United States who have lost faith in republican institutions than at any period since the adoption of the Constitution."[16] But the essays also make use of a Hegelian framework in order to recontextualize this crisis as a potential step toward the actualization of the American spirit. In fact, Snider essentially recasts Hegel's history of civilization as the history of the American republic. In *The Philosophy of History* Hegel interprets world history as the progressive actualization of the principle of free self-determination, a principle that first appears on the world-historical stage in ancient Greece. While Hegel's Greeks were animated by the spirit of free individuality, however, this spirit was a consequence of unreflected custom and thus imperfect; they lacked any consciousness of freedom as a rational principle. The achievement of a self-conscious awareness of freedom as the essence of humanity was left to the Reformation, which, according to Hegel, also began a transformation that would ultimately reshape all social institutions in concordance with human reason. There are of course some important dialectical twists and turns missing from this summary, but it serves to foreground the crucial role of self-consciousness in Hegel's narrative. For Hegel, it is not enough for a society's institutions to operate according to the principle of freedom; true freedom only exists when the members of that society are also consciously aware that this principle constitutes the foundation of their social order. As he puts it, "In Greece, viz., we have the freedom of the individual, but it has not yet advanced to such a degree of abstraction, that the subjective unit is conscious of direct dependence on the [general] substantial principle — the State as such."[17]

This same concern with self-consciousness serves as the organizing principle for the first section of *The American State.* Surprisingly, perhaps, Snider chooses not to present American history as a continuation of Hegel's world-historical narrative. Such a strategy would have been in line with Hegel's own comments on North America, as well as with a range of other evolutionary interpretations of America's historical mission.[18] Snider himself moves in this direction in the latter sections of the pamphlet. His initial description, however, suggests that the evolution of the American republic mirrors the history of spirit *in its entirety.* The first phase of American history is described in terms reminiscent of Hegel's Greece. According to Snider, in the period following the adoption of the Constitution, the country was characterized by a perfect identification between individual and nation. Citizens were filled with national pride, and they knew with the certainty born of experience that their governmental institutions corresponded to their deepest needs. And yet this state of affairs was imperfect, because the endorsement of these institutions remained at the level of instinct. In Snider's words, it was "the period of national childhood," characterized by "the simple ethical faith which questions not, but is in the deepest harmony with truth."[19] As in Hegel's Greece, moreover, this harmony began to disintegrate when individual consciousness came into conflict with national authority. Snider describes this moment as "the contradiction between individual conscience and authority,"[20] and he explains the slow emergence of this contradiction as a consequence of slavery. For both its defenders and its opponents, slavery gave rise to a tension between individuals and their government. What had previously been the object of unreflected affirmation became problematic. Whereas defenders of slavery were prepared to destroy the state in order to uphold a particular social order, opponents of slavery were willing to do the same through their insistence on the inalienable rights of the individual.

Snider refuses to take sides in this discussion, and his reluctance to support the cause of the North in this context is certainly disconcerting. He did in fact condemn slavery, but, like the arguments of many of slavery's opponents in the period, his tended to emphasize questions of principle. The slaves themselves he considered not yet "socially ready" for emancipation.[21] While it is important to recognize these troubling aspects of his thought, more significant for the current argument is the basic framework Snider employs to grasp the national crisis and its aftermath. For Snider, the Civil War represents the great antithesis or negation of American history, which resulted from an inherent contradiction in the organization of the early republic.[22] The institution of slavery stood in opposition to the principle upon which the country was founded and thus threatened to destroy it, but the ensuing crisis has also opened up the possibility of a return to the harmony of the first epoch at a higher level. This new era, which Snider characterizes as "the period of robust manhood," will begin when Americans become conscious of their "national principle," when "instead of the immediate unity between the individual and the government, there arises the higher unity mediated by thought, based not upon the transitory element of feeling, but upon an everlasting foundation, the self-conscious reason of the nation."[23]

In the remainder of the text, Snider attempts to elucidate this principle, an exercise that itself entails an interesting appropriation of the Hegelian theory of government. He shares Hegel's belief that a fully human life is impossible outside of the state. True freedom is not caprice; it is action in accordance with the universal will, and this will can only be realized within an institutional framework.[24] Briefly put, the state for

Snider represents a concretization of rational human will, the sole purpose of which is to secure the conditions for the further exercise of that will. After developing this concept of the state as the "Will which wills Will," he goes on to deduce the necessity of the three branches of government, and more importantly, of a constitutional confederacy, which he views as the ideal form of the state.[25] Such a confederacy represents for Snider the perfect realization of the concept of the state, because it is a state that has the protection of the state as its explicit objective. In other words, the constitutional confederacy exists for the sole purpose of maintaining the integrity of the individual states. As Snider sees it, only one state has emerged over the course of world history that embodies this ideal. It is the United States, which has come into being in order to protect the members of the confederacy it comprises. This purpose constitutes the previously mentioned "national principle" of which Americans must now become conscious. In the period leading up to the Civil War, advocates of secession failed to grasp this principle to the extent that they insisted upon the rights of the individual states without acknowledging that these rights can only be secured as long as the Union remains intact. In the wake of the war the United States is faced with a threat from the opposite direction, namely, the threat of a one-sided valorization of the Union with its corresponding tendency toward a centralization that destroys the individual state. For Snider, this tendency constitutes a historical regression, a return to an absolutist model, which preserves unity but without the possibility of individuality. Both threats are avoidable only insofar as citizens become cognizant of the rational principle upon which their government is founded and use this principle as the basis for their actions.

Snider thus presents the development of the United States in terms that recall Hegel's theory of world-history as a process by which spirit "discovers its true nature and becomes conscious of itself."[26] In the penultimate section of the pamphlet, he supplements his logical deduction of the constitutional confederacy with an empirical demonstration. In seventeen action-packed pages he works his way through Asia, Greece, Rome, and medieval and modern Europe before concluding that this form of government is not only a logical necessity, but that it can also be discerned as the implicit tendency of global development. In Snider's account, then, the evolution of the United States appears both as a recreation of the history of civilization—in the first section—and here, as its culmination. To be sure, he is less than fully confident that the United States will actually achieve the higher state of harmony for which it would seem to be destined. Although he adopts Hegel's conceptual framework, Snider lacks his mentor's certainty regarding the place of reason in history.[27] Nonetheless, the framework itself provides a means for reconciling his belief in an American mission with both the catastrophe of the Civil War and the perceived degeneration of political culture in its aftermath.

But this dilemma is not the only one that Hegel helps to resolve. From the perspective of cultural transfer, Snider's arguments also prove interesting for their implications for the status of the United States vis-à-vis Europe. Snider's emphasis on the Hegelian notion of self-consciousness points to his sense of America's deficient intellectual culture, a deficiency that must be remedied before the country can realize its world-historical destiny. At various points in the text Snider refers to the danger of a purely instinctual patriotism and insists upon the necessity of rational insight into the nature of American government. As he puts it, in terms that sound surprisingly relevant in the current political context, "an intense feeling for country is not enough; patriotism is not knowledge, and hence is likely to destroy the very object which it is seeking."[28] One can discern in such arguments and elsewhere in the essay a subtext of inferiority with regard to European intellectual achievements; indeed, the text itself constitutes an intervention designed to enhance American political theory through the importation of a European intellectual tradition.[29] By the same token, however, Snider uses Hegel's framework as a way to assert America's superiority over Europe, both explicitly and implicitly. He presents the United States as the realization of a world-historical idea and as the culmination of a world-historical development that has left Europe behind. While the United States of America has already become a reality, the United States of Europe remain a hope for the future. He writes, "The deeper consciousness is not yet ripened, the thought of the Constitutional Confederacy is not yet European."[30] America, in other words, offers a glimpse of Europe's future, even if it currently finds itself in a state of total disarray. On a more subtle level, his depiction of United States history as the re-enactment of the history of spirit in its entirety involves an even more ambitious revaluation. Through this rhetorical strategy Snider essentially absorbs Hegel's history of civilization into the history of the United States, which thereby becomes an allegory for the realization of human freedom as such.

Snider is primarily concerned with political corruption in this pamphlet, but his arguments also reflect the widespread dismay among period intellectuals with a general lack of theoretical culture in the United States.[31] The contribution of Hegel's dialectic is thus not simply that it allows Snider to view the Civil War and its aftermath within the framework of a larger narrative of progress, but also that it offers a solution to the problem of America's apparent intellectual inferiority. Concern with this topic surfaces at various points in the St. Louis Hegelians' work, as when Harris, for example, responds to criticisms of the allegedly "Un-American" contents of the *JSP* with the question: "In what books is one to find the true 'American' type of Speculative Philosophy?"[32] Hegel's dialectic allows Snider to have it both ways, to criticize America's intellectual shortcomings while simultaneously viewing these shortcomings as transitory and thus not indicative of a fundamental flaw in character of the republic. If the lack of American cultural and intellectual achievements had long been a source of unease among the country's elites, Hegel's notion of self-consciousness provides Snider with a uniquely compelling explanation for the country's apparently uneven progress. In his description the United States appears as both more and less advanced than Europe—it represents the concrete realization of an ideal, but an ideal of which the citizenry is unaware. By emphasizing the progression from practical political achievements to rational insight into the nature of these achievements, however, Snider manages to turn this very unevenness into a sign of the country's forward momentum. From this perspective as well, then, he is able to maintain his belief in America's world-historical mission.

"English and German"

A remarkably similar constellation of concerns can be found in an essay written by fellow traveler Harris in the same period. It would actually be more appropriate to refer to a series of essays, inasmuch as the author published nearly identical material on at least four separate occasions between 1872 and 1890. The original version was first presented as a lecture entitled "German Reform in American Education" before appearing in *The Western*, the same journal that ran Snider's articles. The content of the essay is rather more ambitious than the modest title would suggest, offering nothing less than a characterization of the country's alleged moral collapse and of the role of education in its resolution. Although Harris has a far more digressive style than Snider, he is concerned with the same developments, and he frames his solution in nearly identical terms. The main difference between the two lies in the fact that whereas Snider's focus is largely institutional, Harris frames his arguments in terms of race. He claims in familiar fashion that "vice and corruption flaunt their hateful colors in the public gaze" and refers to a "generation turning critically back on upon the institutions of their fathers."[33] Moreover, like Snider, he blames this state of affairs on the uncertainty caused by reflection and insists that "our new conventional forms must be of conscious, rational origin."[34] Unlike Snider, however, he inserts this argument into a more comprehensive conceptual framework based on a perceived opposition between two nationalities.

According to Harris, the Anglo-Saxon race has thus far provided the principle according to which the United States has developed. Unfortunately for the country, however, this race lacks all propensity for deep thought. Its strength lies rather in the development of practical institutions, institutions whose historical significance has far transcended the limited conscious awareness that motivated their establishment. As Harris puts it, "[The Anglo-Saxons] secrete laws and conventionalities much as the cane secretes its sugar, or the cotton plant its fibre, or as the unconscious bee builds his cell."[35] As the current immorality has made clear, however, this Anglo-Saxon principle of pure will has exhausted itself: "The development of the *will* side of the Anglo-Saxon peoples, has on this continent unfolded a phase whose only hope of solution lies in the mastery of all-comprehending systems of thought."[36] Such mastery, Harris explains, in a gesture that must have pleased his audience, is a characteristic of the Germans. In a series of descriptions that largely echo the self-characterizations of nineteenth-century German intellectuals, Harris links the Germans to Greek antiquity and emphasizes the profundity and systematicity of German science.[37] He ends this section of the essay with an assertion of the necessity of a greater German influence on the culture of the United States, claiming that "without availing ourselves of German thought and science, we shall grope for a long time in the wilderness."[38]

For Harris, then, Hegel's dialectical progression from unreflected custom to self-conscious principle is mapped onto an opposition between what he views as two races, the German and the Anglo-Saxon.[39] As in Snider's case, Hegel's thought provides a conceptual apparatus that allows him to rationalize both America's alleged moral decline and its lack of a theoretical culture as a merely temporary phase in the development of the nation. In Harris's case, moreover, the identification of intellectuality with the German nation also provides a framework, albeit an exclusionary one, for coming to terms with the increasingly multi-ethnic character of the country. For Harris, the full realization of American potential is only possible to the extent that the country recognizes and incorporates what contemporaries would have termed its "German element."[40] The implication of Harris's argument is that America will eventually achieve a kind of Hegelian *Aufhebung* or sublation, in which the individual characteristics of the two races will be preserved but their one-sidedness overcome.

While his position can hardly be considered progressive from a twenty-first century perspective, Harris's endorsement of the Germans does distinguish him from those contemporaries who insisted upon the exclusively Anglo-Saxon character of the United States. His position is also interesting in that it departs from what might be called the "frontier" paradigm, formulated most memorably by Frederick Jackson Turner in 1893. In Harris's discussion, there is no sense of immigrants becoming "Americanized" through a particular shared experience, because America itself is viewed as an incomplete project. Harris, in other words, sees no pre-existing American national identity to which these immigrants could assimilate. Indeed, in later versions of the essay he presents the frontier experience as the trigger of an atavistic regression rather than the emergence of a new "type." There Harris points out that American cowboys, miners, hunters, and trappers all demonstrate the stubborn individualism characteristic of the Teutonic race. Although he finds this individualism impressive, he nonetheless describes it as "the supremest realization of savagery and barbarism," which is "not sufficient of itself to form a civilization."[41]

Harris's attitude toward the Germans no doubt reflects his own personal experiences—he was born in Massachusetts and educated at Yale before moving to the Germanized cultural milieu of St. Louis, and the discovery of German philosophy marked a turning point in his own intellectual development.[42] But Harris's appropriation of Hegel in this context is clearly also a response to demographic shifts, in particular to the massive influx of German immigrants to the United States between 1830 and 1870, and it reflects a mindset not atypical of residents on the frontier. One gains a sense of this mindset in a published response to an 1887 variant of Harris's essay.[43] The respondent, James MacAlister, explains that while Americans derive a great deal of their character from the English, the recent infusion of Germans has enriched the blood of the country. He then goes on to remark that "the result will doubtless be a different type of man, a different type of mind . . . [and] the fact that the mass of German emigration has found its way to the Mississippi Valley, points to it as the region where this new national type is to be looked for."[44] This sense of the Middle West as the vanguard of a new America receives one of its most striking expressions in a pamphlet written much earlier by Logan Uriah Reavis, a St. Louis publicist and tireless advocate for the city. In 1871 he published a forty-three page letter to President Grant entitled "The National Capital Moveable," in which he argued that the national capital should be transferred to St. Louis.[45]

From the standpoint of America's changing demographics as well, then, Hegel's notion of spirit becoming conscious of itself provides a useful conceptual framework. The dialectic enables Harris to take a potentially unsettling social upheaval and rationalize it as a necessary moment in the country's narrative of progress. But the essay includes yet a further significant subtext that links it to Snider's work. More conspicuously than Snider, Harris is concerned not only with moral and political corruption, but also with America's seeming intellectual underdevelopment, particularly in comparison to Europe. And, like his fellow Hegelian, he constructs his arguments in a manner that allows him both to criticize the United States and to assert its advantages over the Old World. The split between Anglo-Saxon and German contributions to the nation not only implies that the American character is in a state of becoming, but also that both Britain and Germany suffer from one-sidedness. Thus Harris can insist that the United States must appropriate the achievements of these nations without abandoning his belief in the general superiority of his own country, a superiority made possible precisely through its capacity to absorb and combine those achievements.

Later versions of the essay offer an interesting variation on this narrative. Here the Anglo-Saxons and Germans are presented as subgroups within a larger family of European nationalities, all of which are categorized as having "Teutonic" stock. Harris's valorization of the Teutonic must no doubt be viewed as part of the widespread and rather convoluted discourse of racial Anglo-Saxonism in the period, even though he insists on drawing distinctions between German and Anglo-Saxon.[46] While Harris certainly sees important differences between the various European nationalities, he also insists that "Germanic blood" is to be found in all the peoples of Europe, and that this blood distinguishes them from both the peoples of European antiquity and the so-called "savage tribes" from elsewhere in the world.[47] In Harris's narrative the existence of distinctive European national characters is beyond question but always has to be considered against the backdrop of a more basic unity. All of the European nationalities appear as ultimately derivative and inextricably intertwined with one another. They represent a historical fusion of Greek, Roman, Judean, and Teutonic principles, with Romans being Germanized, Germans Romanized, and everybody Christianized under the rule of Charlemagne. With regard to the relative status of the Old versus the New World, Harris's complex dialectic of identity and difference appears as yet another defensive strategy, inasmuch as it suggests an effort to project the multi-ethnic character of the United States back onto Europe. In other words, if Snider presented American history as the reenactment of Hegel's version of the history of Europe, Harris's essay suggests an effort to represent European history in terms of a blending of nationalities at least as complex as that to be found in nineteenth-century America. The consequence is the establishment of a kind of equivalence between the United States and Europe, which preempts any denigration of the former based on its more conspicuously hybrid character.

Harris's texts ultimately raise more questions than they answer. It is by no means clear, for example, whether he conceives the "German contribution" to America as a consequence of racial chemistry or simply the spread of ideas.[48] Related to this ambiguity is his rather slippery treatment, hardly uncommon in the period, of the two nationalities that constitute his focus. The description of the Anglo-Saxon's "secretion" of "laws and conventionalities" suggests a racial-biological conception of the nation, but he does not develop this conception in any detail, and later in the article he discusses the pros and cons of the blending of nationalities in America in purely cultural terms. Finally, the introduction of other nationalities into the mix in later essays raises the question of how seriously we should take the binary opposition between German and Anglo-Saxon or the valorization of the Germans that frames the first version of the essay.

Lest one think the exhortations to Germanize the country are merely a concession to his audience, it is important to recognize the extent to which Harris kept returning to this opposition. I have already mentioned the 1887 version of the essay, but the same arguments appeared in at least two other texts, one published in the *Andover Review* in 1886 and another published as a pamphlet in 1890 with the title *German Instruction in American Schools and the National Idiosyncrasies of the Anglo-Saxons and the Germans.*[49] As late as 1899, in a letter thanking Professor Rudolph Eucken for news of an honorary degree from University of Jena, Harris writes of his belief that "the mission of Germany is to elevate the art of government out of the sway of blind feeling into the clear light of rationality."[50] In his later essays Harris backs away from explicit assertions of America's need to incorporate the German principle of deep thought, perhaps because the practical challenges of integration and debates over bilingual education had made such a position more controversial. Nonetheless, the idea of a historical dialectic remains discernable in these essays, together with the implication that this dialectic finds its resolution in the Anglo-German fusion that defines the United States.

Conclusion

Taken together, these essays by Harris and Snider enrich our understanding of the multifaceted constellation of concerns that Hegel's philosophy, and his dialectic in particular, helped to alleviate in nineteenth-century America. Some of the anxieties expressed here, such as that of national disintegration brought about by the war or of a nation defined exclusively in terms of "brittle individualism," have always figured prominently in discussions of the St. Louis Hegelians.[51] The idea of self-consciousness, however, sheds light on what is arguably the most fundamental concern of all. The claim that the United States must become aware of its own founding principle demonstrates the extent to which Harris and Snider viewed the Civil War and its chaotic aftermath as a consequence of America's intellectual immaturity. From this perspective, not only their appropriation of Hegel but their more general life-long project of disseminating high culture must be seen as a conscious strategy of nation building, one designed to overcome what they saw as a dangerous flaw in the national character. In this context the dialectic appears most significant as a kind of psychological defense mechanism, inasmuch as it permits the St. Louis Hegelians to thematize and address this perceived intellectual immaturity without admitting any permanent inferiority on the part of the United States.

Recognizing the significance of intellectual culture in these texts also helps us map the complex force-field in which their understanding of American nationhood takes shape. At stake in these essays is not merely a reconciliation between Northern and Southern states, or between New England and the Middle West. On the contrary, in their reflections on American identity, the struggle to overcome national disunity is inextricable from efforts to situate the United States within a larger international framework. For Harris and Snider, grasping the impact of the war also involves negotiating the relationship between the United States and Europe, and less obviously, between a vaguely defined, allegedly civilized West and everything else. Their assessments of the state of the union reveal an acute sense of being in competition with Europe, but in a competition that assumes the character of a sibling rivalry as soon as non-European cultures enter into the equation.

It has become something of a commonplace to insist on the impossibility of conceiving national cultures in isolation. As one well-known commentator has put it, "Cultures are never unitary in themselves, nor simply dualistic in relation of Self to Other."[52] In the case of the United States, much attention has been paid recently to the conflicting conceptions of the nation propagated by immigrant groups prior to the First World War, especially in the West.[53] The essays by Snider and Harris shed light on some of the specificities of the multilayered, sometimes contradictory intercultural context in which reflections on American identity occur in the period—English versus German, American versus European, the "civilized world" versus its various others.

They also illuminate the strategies used to come to terms with these contradictions, and in so doing they reveal one of the more troubling ambiguities of a Hegelian approach to the nation. In some respects, Snider's and Harris's reflections on what it means to be an American are admirably inclusive. Neither has recourse to those claims of mythical origins or unitary "national essences" that have been associated with more negative incarnations of modern nationalism. At the heart of their vision for America is a conception of the ideal state and its citizens based upon the future realization of allegedly universal principles. In this regard they must be seen as part of that intellectual tradition that insists upon America's unique status as an "ideas nation," one where citizenship is open to all who adhere to a particular core of liberal values.[54] As their essays also demonstrate, however, when combined with Hegel's philosophy of history, such a conception can quite easily be made compatible with the exclusion of certain groups. This is because for Hegel the primary agent of history, the nation, is a category that inseparably fuses human collectivities with particular principles or ideas. Nations, according to Hegel, are "the concepts which the spirit has formed of itself."[55]

A similar fusion can be seen in the work of Harris and Snider, as for example in Harris's claim that "the *principle* of individual personality . . . is peculiar to the Teutonic race and *runs in our own veins*" [my emphasis].[56] Despite their emphasis on rational insight and democracy, then, the essays by Snider and Harris exhibit a conflation of intellectual and racialist arguments about national identity that also has a long tradition in American thought and that becomes particularly pernicious in the final decades of the century.[57] The fact that Hegel's philosophy helped to legitimate such conflations must be counted as one of the philosopher's more dubious contributions to nineteenth-century American culture.

Notes

1. William Torrey Harris, "Do the signs of the times indicate a degeneration of American character? A view on the 'negative' side of the question," undated, William Torrey Harris Papers, Missouri Historical Society, St. Louis, Mo. Although the manuscript is undated, it was clearly written before the war, and the Yale College stationery suggests that it was written prior to 1857. The statistics quoted in the essay match up closely with those of the 1850 census.

2. Ibid.

3. The details of this meeting are rather sketchy. Harris's version can be found in the preface to his book, *Hegel's Logic: A Book on the Genesis of the Categories of the Mind* (Chicago: S. C. Griggs and Company, 1895), xii-xiii. An unattributed citation of Brokmeyer's recollection is reprinted in William Schuyler, "German Philosophy in St. Louis," *The Bulletin of the Washington University Association* 2 (1904): 66–67.

4. For an overview of the various phases of this ill-fated undertaking, see John O. Riedl, "The Hegelians of St. Louis, Missouri and their Influence in the United States," in *The Legacy of Hegel: Proceedings of the Marquette Hegel Symposium 1970*, ed. J. J. O'Malley, et al. (The Hague: Martinus Nijhoff, 1973), 268–87.

5. The activities of the St. Louis Hegelians must be understood within the context of a more general efflorescence of intellectual and cultural movements in St. Louis in the late nineteenth century. In addition to the St. Louis Philosophical Society, the focus of which was by no means limited to Hegel, a number of other clubs and societies were founded in the period. Among the more significant were the Kant Club (1874), which was founded by Harris and also studied Hegel; the Aristotle Club (1873); the Shakespeare Society (1870); and the St. Louis Art Society (1866). See Henry A. Pochmann, *German Culture in America: Philosophical and Literary Influences, 1600-1900* (Madison: University of Wisconsin Press, 1957), 289-90. For a description of the Art Society, see Kurt Leidecker, *Yankee Teacher: The Life of William Torrey Harris* (New York: The Philosophical Library, 1946), 299–307.

6. Loyd D. Easton has documented the history and thought of J. B. Stallo, Peter Kaufmann, Moncure Conway, and August Willich (the "Ohio Hegelians"), who were already disseminating Hegelian ideas a decade prior to the emergence of the St. Louis group. See Easton, *Hegel's First American Followers* (Athens: Ohio University Press, 1966). Hegel had also been presented to an American audience in works like James Murdock, *Sketches of Modern Philosophy especially among the Germans* (Hartford, Conn.: J. C. Wells, 1846), in which the author refers to Hegel as the "most unintelligible writer" he has ever read (120), and in Frederick Henry Hedge, *Prose Writers of Germany* (Philadelphia: Carey and Hart, 1847). For a discussion of the influence of these works, see William Goetzmann, ed., *The American Hegelians: An*

Intellectual Episode in the History of Western America (New York: Alfred A. Knopf, 1973), 3–18.

7. For a list of Snider's publications, see Arthur E. Bostwick, "List of Books Written by Denton J. Snider, Litt. D. with Annotations," *St. Louis Public Library Monthly Bulletin* 22, no. 5 (1924): 102–8. Henry R. Evans compiled a list of Harris's publications for the Bureau of Education that was published in 1908. It has been reprinted in Charles Milton Perry, *The St. Louis Movement in Philosophy: Some Source Material* (Norman: University of Oklahoma Press, 1930), 96–148.

8. The following remark by James A. Good can be considered representative: "The St. Louis Hegelians were most attracted to Hegel's thought as a philosophy of cultural and national unification" (Good, "A 'World-Historical Idea': The St. Louis Hegelians and the Civil War," *Journal of American Studies* 34, no. 3 [2000]: 450).

9. Hegel, *The Philosophy of History*, trans. J. Sibree (New York: Dover Publications, 1956), 86.

10. Harvey Gates Townsend, "The Political Philosophy of Hegel in a Frontier Society," in Edward L. Schaub, ed., *William Torrey Harris (1835-1935): A Collection of Essays, Including Papers and Addresses Presented in Commemoration of Dr. Harris' Centennial at the St. Louis Meeting of the Western Division of the American Philosophical Society* (Chicago: The Open Court Publishing Company, 1936), 76.

11. Goetzmann, *American Hegelians,* 15.

12. See, for example, Francis Harmon, *The Social Philosophy of the St. Louis Hegelians* (New York: n.p., 1943), 1–2, and Elizabeth Flower and Murray G. Murphey, *A History of Philosophy in America* (New York: G. P. Putnam's Sons, 1977), 2:502.

13. Good, "'World-Historical Idea,'" 447–64.

14. Denton Snider, *The St. Louis Movement in Philosophy, Literature, Education, Psychology* (St. Louis: Sigma Publishing Co., 1920), 70–116; 134. See also Pochmann, *German Culture,* 268.

15. For a discussion, see Pochmann, *German Culture*, 264–65. Snider published more than fifty books during his lifetime, virtually all of them with his own publishing house, Sigma Publishing Co.

16. Denton Snider, *The American State* (1874; reprinted as an appendix in Snider, *The State, Specially the American State, Psychologically Treated* [St. Louis: Sigma Publishing Co., 1902]), 497.

17. Hegel, *Philosophy of History*, 250–51.

18. See, for example, Reginald Horsman, *Race and Manifest Destiny: The Origins of American Racial Anglo-Saxonism* (Cambridge: Harvard University Press, 1981), especially chapter five, and Merle Curti, *The Growth of American Thought* (New York: Harper & Row, 1964), 552–60.

19. Snider, *The American State*, 505.

20. Snider, *The American State*, 505.

21. In making his arguments, Snider also draws upon Hegel's famous master-slave dialectic from *The Phenomenology of Spirit* (Good, "World-Historical Idea," 460). See also Snider, *The American Ten Years War, 1855-1865* (St. Louis: Sigma Publishing Co., 1906), 321–23.

22. Harmon, *Social Philosophy*, 62.

23. Snider, *The American State*, 508.

24. Harris also makes this point repeatedly. In the first volume of the *JSP*, for example, he writes, "Now we [American citizens] have arrived at the consciousness of the other essential phase, and each individual recognizes his substantial side to be the State as such. The freedom of the citizen does not consist in the mere Arbitrary, but in the realization of the rational conviction which finds expression in established law" ("To the Reader," *JSP* 1, no. 1 [1867]: 1).

25. Snider offers a much more elaborate and somewhat less obviously Hegelian version of this deduction in his *The State, Specially the American State, Psychologically Treated* (St. Louis: Sigma, 1902). For a summary, see Harmon, *Social Philosophy*, 50–68.

26. Hegel, *Lectures on the Philosophy of World History*, trans. H. B. Nisbet (Cambridge: Cambridge University Press, 1975), 65.

27. Snider's uncertainty casts doubt on Francis Harmon's claim that the St. Louis philosophers had greater faith in progress than Hegel (*Social Philosophy*, 100). But Harmon is certainly correct to claim that their thought had "a strongly voluntaristic stamp" (7).

28. Snider, *The American State*, 519.

29. In his 1920 autobiography *cum* history of the St. Louis Movement, Snider comments on the tension inherent in the group's appropriation of European high culture. He writes, "Hence arose the fifth cultural element [characteristic of St. Louis], homegrown, distinctive, sprung of the time and the city's native character; this we called our own St. Louis Movement, which never failed to assert its prime originality. And yet it too was based upon Tradition; it prescribed a European philosopher and his philosophy just to attack and supplant European prescription" (Snider, *The St. Louis Movement*, 223).

30. Snider, *The American State*, 554.

31. To give just one example, in an 1847 "editor's address" in the *Massachusetts Quarterly Review*, Ralph Waldo Emerson expresses his fear that "there is nothing colossal in the country but its geography and its material activities; that the moral and intellectual efforts are not on the same scale with the trade and production" (*The Complete Works of Ralph Waldo Emerson*, ed. Edward Waldo Emerson [Boston: Houghton, Mifflin, and Company, 1904], 11:385). The seminal European work in this context is Tocqueville's *Democracy in America* (1835/40), the second volume of which links American underachievement in philosophy, science, and the arts to the effects of democracy. The German historian von Treitschke offers a more temporally proximate example in his 1864 description of the United States: "And this has remained characteristic of American life: a generally high level of prosperity and cultivation . . . but also a preponderance of intellectual mediocrity, a prosaic and sober view

of life, of the sort embodied by Benjamin Franklin, and the restriction of the state to provision of the most basic necessities." Quoted in Ernst Fraenkel, ed., *Amerika im Spiegel des deutschen politischen Denkens* (Cologne: Westdeutscher Verlag, 1959), 120 (my translation).

32. William Torrey Harris, "Preface," *JSP* 1, no. 1 (1867): i. In the same year, T. W. Higginson published a "Plea for Culture" in the *Atlantic Monthly*, in which he argued that America needed to create cultural institutions on a par with European models. See Frank Trommler, "Literary Scholarship and Ethnic Studies," in Winfried Fluck and Werner Sollors, eds., *German? American? Literature?: New Directions in German-American Studies* (New York: Peter Lang, 2002), 29.

33. William Torrey Harris, "German Reform in American Education," *The Western* 3 (1872): 327.

34. Ibid., 328.

35. Ibid., 327.

36. Ibid., 327.

37. Harris's characterization of the Greeks as a "transcendent people," however, does not in fact correspond to Hegel's characterization in the *Philosophy of History*.

38. Harris, "German Reform in American Education," 328.

39. Harris appears to have taken this opposition from Brokmeyer. In a transcription of Brokmeyer's lectures on Goethe's *Faust*, Harris writes, "The German wills through knowing. . . . The Englishman knows through will" ("Goethe's Faust—an abstract of lectures on the same delivered by H. C. Brokmeyer, February and March 1865 at his office on 3rd St," 1865, William Torrey Harris Papers, Missouri Historical Society, St. Louis, Mo.).

40. The best known use of this phrase is in the work by A. B. Faust, *The German Element in the United States* (Boston: Houghton Mifflin, 1909).

41. William Torrey Harris, "What is Most Valuable to Us in German Philosophy and Literature," in Marion V. Dudley, ed., *Poetry and Philosophy of Goethe* (Chicago: S. C. Griggs and Company, 1887), 229.

42. See Leidecker, *Yankee Teacher*, esp. 132-40.

43. Harris, "German Philosophy and Literature," 246-49.

44. Ibid., 248.

45. L. U. Reavis, *The National Capital Movable. A letter to President Grant on the Subject of the Removal of the National Capital* (St. Louis: Missouri Democrat Book and Job Printing House, 1971). Reavis's other well-known text, *St. Louis the Future Great City of the World,* was printed in both English and German and was apparently subsidized by the city government. See Snider, *The St. Louis Movement*, 86.

46. See Horsman, *Race and Manifest Destiny*, especially chapters five through nine.

47. William Torrey Harris, "English and German," *The Andover Review* 7 (1886): 596-97. He appears to use the terms *Germanic* and *Teutonic* synonymously.

48. Harris, "German Reform," 326.

49. William Torrey Harris, *German Instruction in American Schools and the National Idiosyncrasies of the Anglo-Saxons and the Germans. Delivered Before the National German American Teachers' Association at Cleveland, Ohio, July 16th, 1890* (n.p., n.d.).

50. Letter of Harris to Eucken, March 8, 1899, William Torrey Harris Papers, Missouri Historical Society, St. Louis, Mo.

51. Harris, "To the Reader," *JSP* 1, no. 1 (1867): 1.

52. Homi Bhabha, "Cultural Diversity and Cultural Differences," in Bill Ashcroft, et al., eds., *The Postcolonial Studies Reader* (London: Routledge, 1995), 207.

53. See, for example, Jon Gjerde, *The Minds of the West: Ethnocultural Evolution in the Rural Middle West, 1830-1917* (Chapel Hill: University of North Carolina Press, 1997).

54. As Nathan Glazer put it in 1993, "[W]e are a nation based not on a common ethnic stock linked by mystic cords of memory, connection, kinship, but rather by common universal ideas" (Glazer, "The Closing Door," *The New Republic*, December 27, 1993, 17).

55. Hegel, *Lectures on the Philosophy of World History*, 51.

56. Harris, "English and German," 596.

57. For a comprehensive analysis of this tradition from a legal perspective, see Rogers Smith, *Civic Ideals: Conflicting Visions of Citizenship in U.S. History* (New Haven: Yale University Press, 1997). A discussion of developments toward the end of the century can be found in William Petersen, et al., *Concepts of Ethnicity* (Cambridge: Harvard University Press, 1982), 79–109.

Contributors

Britt-Marie Schiller is professor and chair of the Philosophy Department at Webster University in St. Louis. Her research and publications are mainly in the areas of gender and psychoanalytic theories.

Doug Anderson teaches in the Philosophy Department at Southern Illinois University–Carbondale. He focuses on American philosophy and the history of philosophy, and is author of two books and numerous essays dealing with issues in American philosophy and culture. A number of these essays deal with the philosophy of sport and the theory of physical education. His most recent book is *Philosophy Americana* from Fordham University Press.

Matt Erlin is associate professor of German and humanities at Washington University in St. Louis. He is the author of *Berlin's Forgotten Future: City, History, and Enlightenment In Eighteenth-Century Germany* (2004). His is also the co-editor, together with Lynne Tatlock, of *German Culture in Nineteenth-Century America: Reception, Adaptation, Transformation* (2005), and he has published articles on a variety of topics related to late-eighteenth- and early nineteenth-century German culture. His current research investigates the discourse of luxury in the German Enlightenment and its relevance for the emergence of new conceptions of literature and aesthetic experience in the period.

James Good is a professor of history and chair of the Department of Social Sciences at Lone Star College–North Harris in Houston, Texas. His research focuses on the American reception of German idealism. He is the author of numerous articles on American intellectuals, such as the St. Louis Hegelians, the Ohio Hegelians, and John Dewey, and has edited republications of the writings of many more American intellectuals. He is also the author of *A Search for Unity in Diversity: The "Permanent Hegelian Deposit" in the Philosophy of John Dewey* (2006).

Dorothy Rogers is the author of *America's First Women Philosophers: Transplanting Hegel*, and has edited or co-edited several collections of the works of women philosophers, including Catharine Beecher, the women of the St. Louis Philosophical Movement, and early women philosophers in the American academy (1880-1900). She served as the coordinating editor for entries on women for the *Dictionary of Modern American Philosophers* and is currently serving the same role for the upcoming *Dictionary of Early American Philosophers*, both published by Thoemmes Press. She teaches philosophy and women's studies at Montclair State University in New Jersey, where she is an associate professor and chair of the Department of Philosophy and Religion. She is currently exploring the connections between feminism, altruism, and pacifism in political life.

Jerome P. Schiller is an emeritus professor of philosophy at Washington University in St. Louis. He taught at Washington from 1963 to 1999, specializing in ancient philosophy. His research has been in aesthetics and ancient philosophy and includes a book in the former field, *I. A. Richards' Theory of Literature* (Yale U. P., 1960), and several articles in the latter field in such journals as *Phronesis*, *Journal of the History of Philosophy*, and *Apeiron*.

LaVergne, TN USA
30 October 2009
162427LV00005B/10/P